POETICA *32*

YEHUDA HALEVI · POEMS FROM THE DIWAN

by Gabriel Levin

POETRY

Sleepers of Beulah
Ostraca

TRANSLATIONS

The Little Bookseller Oustaz Ali
by Ahmed Rassim
Never Mind: Twenty Poems and a Story
by Taha Muhammad Ali
(with Peter Cole and Yahya Hijazi)

Yehuda Halevi

Poems
from the Diwan

TRANSLATED AND INTRODUCED BY
Gabriel Levin

ANVIL PRESS POETRY

Published in 2002
by Anvil Press Poetry Ltd
Neptune House 70 Royal Hill London SE10 8RF
www.anvilpresspoetry.com

This book is published with financial assistance
from The Arts Council of England

Designed and set in Monotype Bell by Anvil

ISBN 0 85646 333 7

A catalogue record for this book
is available from the British Library

Acknowledgments

Early versions of some of the translations in this collection appeared in the following periodicals and anthologies: *Ariel*, *The Jerusalem Post*, *The Jerusalem Anthology: A Literary Guide*, *The Jerusalem Review*, *European Judaism*, *PN Review*, *Tikkun*, *The Times Literary Supplement*, *World Poetry: An Anthology of Verse From Antiquity To Our Time* (Norton, 1998). The sequence of poems "On the Sea" first appeared as *On The Sea* (Ibis Editions, 1997). "In Alexandria" appeared in *Ostraca* (Anvil, 1999).

I am especially grateful to Zali Gurevitch for guiding me through the Hebrew. I would also like to thank Peter Cole, Jennie Feldman, Varda and Harold Schimmel, Jeremy Schonfield, Elchanan Reiner, and Joseph Yahalom.

Contents

Introduction   9

A Sleepless Night   35
Cheated   36
A Reminder   37
To Shlomo Ibn al-Muallim   38
Wake Up from Your Slumber   39
Graceful Doe, Pity This Heart   40
A Small Consolation   41
Elegy for a Child   42
In Praise of Shlomo Ibn Ghiyyat   43
After Mutanabbi   46
Three Bridal Songs   47
The Fawn   49
To Yitzhak the Orphan (Ibn Elitom)   50
Ophra Washes Her Clothes   52
Why Sweetheart Keep Your Envoys   53
Bear Arms Against the Victim   56
On Parting from his Friend Moshe Ibn Ezra   57
Wine Songs   60
The Night My Doe   61
To Shlomo Ibn Feruziel upon Returning
    from Aragon   62
Riddles   64
Impromptu   65
The Sons of Fortune   66
In Praise of Abu al-Hassan Shmuel Ibn Muriel   67
In Seville   69
Now I've Become a Burden   71
A Young Girl's Lament from the Grave   72
Colloquy   75
Distant Dove   76
Solomon's Pavilions   77

Admonitions   78
I Run Towards the Fountain of True Life .   81
You Who Knew Me   82
My Soul Craves   83
The Penitent   84
A Lovely Doe   85
Preciously Abiding   86
Elohi, How Lovely is Your Dwelling   87
Heal Me, My God, and I Will be Healed   88
How My Eyes Shine   89
May My Sweet Songs   90
I Lay My Desire   91
Revelation   93
You Who are Acquainted with Faith   94
Asleep in the Wings of Wandering   95
The Bride Who Longs for You   97
The World was Set Apart   98
Startled Awake   99
Zion, Won't You Ask   100
Earth's Delight and Sovereign City   103
Can Lifeless Bodies   104
Primed for Flight   108
My Heart is in the East   110
On the Sea   111
Egypt   121
To His Friend and Host Ibn al-Ammani   122
Fate Has Flung Me   124
In Alexandria   125

Notes   127

Introduction

His forehead is a sail, his limbs are oars
to set his soul adrift in his body toward Jerusalem

YEHUDA AMICHAI

YEHUDA HALEVI'S NAME had a way of traveling before him. When the elderly Hebrew-Andalusian poet, bound for the Holy Land, sailed into Alexandria in 1140, a huge admiring crowd pressed at the harbor to catch a glimpse of the man whose poems were read from Spain to Yemen, and who had written: "My heart is in the east and I'm at the far end of the west./How can I taste or savor what I eat?"

But even as a young man, soon after leaving his native Tudela in the north and slowly making his way south to al-Andalus, Halevi's name must have kindled enthusiasm, or at least curiosity, in literary circles.[1] Moshe Ibn Ezra, Andalusia's most prominent Hebrew poet at the time, received from the young aspirant an epistle cast in rhymed prose and accompanied by a splendid, monorhymed *qasida*. Ibn Ezra was so impressed by the young poet's accomplished style that he urged Halevi to come to Granada – the seat of Andalusian arts and letters – and lodge in his home. "A light has risen from Seir [Christian Spain]," Ibn Ezra exclaimed in his own verse epistle responding to Halevi. And the poet once again wrote to Ibn Ezra, this time sending a *muwashshah*, an elaborately rhymed strophic poem with a concluding couplet in Romance dialect, composed – so Halevi reveals in the accompanying letter – as a challenge between poets during a literary gathering in one of the towns where he had been invited to stay. Halevi's *muwashshah* perfectly imitates, as was the custom, the thematic progression, meter and rhymes of another Hebrew *muwashshah* (itself an imitation of an Arabic *muwashshah*) composed by the well-known Cordovan, Yosef Ibn Zaddiq. The poet sings the praises of wine; he then delicately alludes to the hidden, absent addressee (Moshe Ibn Ezra), and concludes with an erotic elaboration on the theme of wisdom personified and lured by the beloved. Halevi was showing off his skills with supreme confidence, even though in his letter to Ibn Ezra he spoke of himself as being "slow of speech", as was perhaps fit, the poet adds, for one raised in the north. It must have been during this period too that Halevi sent a poem of praise to another Granada-based poet, Yehuda Ibn Ghiyyat, son of a famed liturgical poet, Isaac Ibn Ghiyyat of Lucena, who promptly responded in kind, alluding in his verses to the poet's northern origins, as did Ibn Ezra, in biblical terms: "Who comes from Edom with dream-thoughts / and robs me of sleep and takes my surety?"

And so Halevi – possibly still in his teens – arrived in Granada, a city famed for the competitive allure of its court life and the excellence of its poets, and sang for his bread, not unlike the troubadours of Provence, before an upper class of urban Jews who spoke Arabic and a patois consisting of a mixture of Arabic and Romance, but used Hebrew for religious study, prayer and – since the tenth century – the writing of secular poetry. Jewish court life, like its Muslim and Christian counterparts, revolved around an intellectual elite of merchants and landholders, physicians and religious scholars, grammarians and lexicographers, advisers, translators, civil servants, and ambassadors-at-large who maintained ties with the various ethnic communities of Spain. Andalusia was a place of remarkable cultural and multilingual confluence where serious study and a broad humanistic approach to learning went hand in hand with a complex aesthetics of leisure. A heightened sense of the transient, sensory world and the concomitant attention to the formal properties of experience permeated all aspects of court life, while political intrigue and the dangers of internecine warfare between city-states hovered in the background.

Since Halevi – or Abu l-Hassan Ibn Hallewi, as his Arab compatriots called him – was writing at the tail-end of the golden age of Andalusian poetry, the ground rules were already clearly set and the range of genres at his disposal was extensive. Alongside the *piyyut*, or liturgical poem written for synagogue recital, any poet of worth was expected to show his skill in the writing of panegyrics, wine poems, bridal songs, boast poems, poems of friendship, laments, wisdom poems, invectives, and, perhaps most notably, lyrics of desire in which hyperbole was modulated by the precise management of diction and tone of voice. Such lyrics stood independently or else formed the erotic prelude to a panegyric-like *qasida*. They were, moreover, frequently addressed to the *zvi* or *ayala* ("fawn" or "doe"), epithets designating the elusive figure of the male or female beloved:

> Easy, my firm-hearted, tender-hipped one,
>> gently now, and I'll bow before you.
> My eyes alone are ravished by your sight.
>> Surely my intentions are pure, but not my eyes.
> Let them gather from your features
>> roses and lilies sown together.
> I'll rake the embers of your cheeks, quenching fire
>> with fire, and when thirsty find
> water there. I'll suck your coal-hot lips,
>> my jaws like tongs – for life
> hangs between their scarlet threads,
>> and my death is twilit . . .

These lines form the opening of a long panegyric to Shlomo Ibn al-Muallim. Its homo-erotic content, however, can be properly understood only once one realizes that the initial addressee is not al-Muallim but rather the standard figure of idealized beauty, more of a type than a real person and frequently represented as a young male wine-bearer. The lines that follow make this abundantly clear, as Halevi now shifts his attention to describing, with just as much rhetorical flair, the elegance and craftsmanship of his friend's handwriting (which exceeds the beauty of the *zvi*): "Rows of flowing myrrh richly embroidered/resemble dusklight at noon,/even Bezalel couldn't have stitched so well/and might have asked Shlomo to lend a hand./The hands that adorned the parchment surpass/in skill those which rouged the gazelle's face."

Halevi's early secular, court poems, however conscious of their own literary code, invariably added a religious flavor, albeit muted, to even the most mundane of observations, whether depicting the beloved "gazelle", or the glass of wine raised for a toast in the company of friends: "The wineglass purifies/the wine's ruddiness – even rubies/are put to shame by its coral glow./It beholds and keeps secret the splendor of its vintage/until it can no longer conceal it./But wine imbibed banishes all my troubles;/this is the sign of the covenant/drawn up between us." For Halevi's poems, in keeping with his times, were woven out of intact or delicately modified biblical citations, called *shibbuts* by modern scholars [see introduction to Notes]. Thus in the above-quoted poem the concealed properties of the wine are compared, by alluding to Exodus 11.1–3, to the hidden power of the infant Moses, and the wine's soothing effects are like the sign of the covenant (Genesis 9.12).

The poets of Andalusia prided themselves on the formal play of poetry. Technical virtuosity, the use of ornate figures of speech, verbal acuity, and aural punning, or paronomasia, were prerequisites for a successful poem. The judicious use of biblical citations served to hone the poetry to a fine double edge. *Shibbuts* functioned simultaneously as a vehicle of delight – a celebration of collective memory – and as a counterbalancing weight. What Franz Rosenzweig has called "the constant pressure of scriptures" provided an undertone of gravity and linguistic purity crucial to a society that straddled religious and ethnic divisions, even while more conservative forces within its establishment constantly questioned the legitimacy of using the Holy Tongue in a non-religious context.

Halevi's early days in Granada could not have lasted long, perhaps two or three years at the most, as in 1090 the city was ransacked by the Almoravid, a Berber brotherhood from North Africa newly converted to Islam. The Almoravid take-over heralded the end of the small Taifa states and the replacement of what one literary historian has called the "chaotically tolerant party kings" by a new military elite intent on spreading its own zealous version of Islam. What remained of the Jewish community fled north. Halevi too left his adopted city, sojourning in Seville and Lucena (it was in the latter city that he may have served for a short period as secretary to Joseph Ibn Migash, head of its yeshiva) before finally settling in the newly "Christianized" Toledo, where he remained for close to twenty years. A letter from the same period attests to his having worked as a physician, perhaps in the court of Alphonso VI:

> Thus I busy myself at an hour that is neither day nor night with the vanities of medicine . . . The city is large and its inhabitants are giants and they are hard masters; and how can a slave please his masters other than by spending his days fulfilling their desires. We heal Babel, but it is beyond healing.

In 1108, Christian mercenaries murdered Halevi's close friend Shlomo Ibn Feruziel. A year later violence erupted in Toledo in the wake of the death of Alfonso VI. Halevi once again turned south where Almoravid rule, succumbing to the appeal of Andalusian life, had tempered its religious militancy. He settled in Cordoba, the "Pearl of Andalusia", which at the time also happened to be the home of the dissolute Ibn Quzman, master of the Hispano-Arabic *zajal* and one of the great poets of medieval Islam. For the next thirty years Halevi was to remain in Cordoba. He was by this time, it should be noted, well established not only as a poet, but also as a public figure with close ties to the leading rabbinic scholars and Jewish community leaders throughout Spain.

In contrast to numerous court poets who were dependent on the good graces of their patron and whose movements were frequently dictated by the need to seek out new patronage, Halevi led a life of economic security as he continued to practice medicine. There is also evidence, found in his correspondence with the Cairene businessman, scholar and traveler, Abu Said Halfon Ibn Natanel Halevi al-Dimyati, that Halevi might have engaged on occasion in some form of trade. It was in Cordoba, so tradition has it, that he wrote the majority of his devotional poems as well as his part polemic, part religio-philosophical treatise, *The Kuzari*, before embarking on his fateful voyage to Egypt and the Holy Land.

SUFFUSED WITH warmth, moving easily between the mundane and the otherworldly, and, above all, delicately elegiac, the poet's voice cuts across all the literary genres and religious modes on which he drew. As Halevi witnessed the final dissolution of the small city-states of Andalusia in the south and the conquest of the north by Christian armies, partings, sudden leave-takings, the "lessons of goodbyes", as Mandelstam would write closer to our own times, were re-enacted with poignant urgency:

> A sleepless night in which the hours hang heavy.
>   Friends leave tomorrow. Night, lead on softly
> and spread your raven wings over dawn's first rays.
>   My tears, raining down on their carriage,
> delay their journey; a cloud, raised by my sulking heart
>   veils the break of day from their sight.
> If only my sighs would turn to smoke and blaze
>   into a scorching fire, hampering their departure
> from my tent, at least until I give my consent.

The Hebrew language was like "soft wax in his hands", wrote the preeminent Hebrew poet of the modern era, Haim Nachman Bialik: "There is no end to the combinations that R. Yehuda renewed in the language, and the richness of its patterns and meters, their variety and multiplicity of forms dazzle the heart." Halevi was undoubtedly adept at composing verse in a wide variety of forms. But technical mastery in adopting into Hebrew Arabic-Andalusian loanwords, motifs, rhetorical devices, and metrical patterns was not uncommon in Halevi's day.[2] By absorbing transposed Arabic literary conventions, Hebrew poetry underwent what Samuel Stern has called a complete "alchemical transmutation". The Hebrew courts of Cordoba, Seville, Lucena, and Granada were there to provide serious entertainment for the intellectual elite. Craft and polish were a prerequisite, as well as a radical sense of doubleness: by using the scriptural word in a wholly new, secular context, the Hebrew poets of Andalusia appeared to be both upholding and subverting their own religious-literary tradition, while at the same time proving to their Muslim counterparts that biblical Hebrew could be just as pure and poetically potent as koranic Arabic.

The poet's immediate predecessors, Shmuel HaNagid, Shlomo Ibn Gabirol, and Moshe Ibn Ezra – the great luminaries of medieval Hebrew poetry – were all consummately skilled at reshaping and revitalizing the Hebrew language with seeming effortlessness. To HaNagid's wisdom and worldly vigor, Ibn Gabirol's mood shifts and imploded cosmology, and Ibn Ezra's rueful melancholy, was now added Halevi's signature longing and compassion. The tone is intimate, reverential, and almost always humble, whether Halevi is speaking lightheartedly of being struck by the good looks of his "doe", lamenting the all too frequent parting of friends, or delving into the mysteries of God's ways. Halevi may have been, moreover, keenly aware of his own poetic belatedness. He came at the twilight of an era and was, particularly in his early courtly poems, the exemplary refiner, rather than innovator, of a tradition. Hence, possibly, the humility in the poet's tone. An early *qasida* addressed to Shlomo Ibn Ghiyyat is quite explicit on the matter:

Here is the fruit of song from your friend
yielding its harvest every month, though love ripens
    continually –
he's come as the best of times draw to an end
and can only stare into the past.
He's one of the invited – and though his name is
    unrecorded
tradition proudly amends for his lateness.
He chases after the noble, clings to their counsel,
they are the lion – and he the tail . . .

Ibn Ghiyyat is one of the many friends, poets, and nota-
bles with whom Halevi corresponded in verse. Halevi's
poems of friendship – far more numerous than comparable
lyrics by his contemporaries – are singularly moving, even
though the modern reader must make allowances and learn
how to read through and across the hyperbole, rhetorical
figuration and verbal arabesque that lie at the heart of
medieval Arabic and Hebrew poetry. Camaraderie offered
the greatest of consolations for life's vicissitudes, "the daily
surge of events", and yet, not unexpectedly, such consola-
tions were undermined by a gnawing sense of the fragility of
relationships; it is this very sense of human instability, and of
the devastating effects of separation, that repeatedly surfaces
in the poetry addressed to friends and patrons, poets, schol-
ars and *payytanim* (liturgical poets). After Moshe Ibn Ezra's
reluctant departure and exile in northern Spain, Halevi
writes with restrained anguish to his long-time friend and
mentor: "Will I ever be the same in your absence?/Wander
and my heart wanders after you." And again, writing to
Moshe's brother Yitzhak, residing in Granada: "Bear greet-
ings to my soul's desire/then seize his answer and breathe it
into the slain/by partings that he may live again."

HALEVI'S EXTENSIVE body of devotional poems, composed for each of the Jewish holy days, recalls above all the poetry of Herbert and Traherne in its metaphysical grace. What makes for an especially variegated and vital body of work is the fact that medieval Hebrew-Andalusian poets saw no inherent contradiction either in alternating between sacred and secular poetry, or in frequently blurring the two genres. Hence a poem by Halevi written specifically for synagogue recitation, as a prelude to the early morning blessing, opens:

> Have you forgotten, love, how you lay in my arms?
>   Why have you sold me for good
> to my oppressors, when it was I who pursued you
>   through barren tracts of land?

There is precedence in Hebrew for such poetry whose origins may very well go back to early midrashic interpretations of the Song of Songs, and which extends through a rich Middle Eastern – and particularly Muslim – tradition of rendering religious texts in the language of erotic courtship. Rooted in Byzantine Palestine, the liturgical lyric rapidly spread to the Jewish communities of Babylonia, and from there to Spain, where it was most successfully reinvigorated: traditional themes of Israel's longing for redemption, of sin and atonement, of exile, captivity, exodus and revelation, were now poured into the new Andalusian "secular" molds and renegotiated within the context of a sophisticated, personalized aesthetic.

Thus "The Penitent", actually a translation of a ninth-century Arabic love poem, employs the conventional figure of the jilted lover to convey a sense of extreme religious contrition in the face of a divine being who has all the attributes of the desirable yet hard-hearted beloved, or "fawn", of courtly love poetry: "Ever since you were love's encampment/my love has camped wherever you dwelled./I delighted for your sake in my rivals' rebuke –/let them be, as they torment the one/you've tormented..." The strophic *muwashshah*, previously used for the writing of urbane, erotic poems which ended with a particularly racy tail-piece, is now transfigured into a vehicle of reverence and ritual confession:

> Asleep in the wings of wandering,
>   slumbering at the ends
> of captivity, all glory spent, I abide
>   in a troubled, sullen heart
>   yet heart restored
>   to the gazelle, my spirits revive,
>   cast off rags of bondage,
>   and dress up in pride; my love within,
>   I've no use for solid
>   ground, or circuit.

It would be unfair, however, to credit Halevi's success with the *piyyut* solely to the loosening of its framework by the skilful introduction of secular forms and courtly imagery, or to its assimilation of novel midrashic readings of scriptures. The transformation in the work runs deeper. Feeling and thought, conviction and craft, converge in the poet's profoundly religious temperament to offer an unfettered vision of a higher good. The poems burst their bounds even as they retain their metrical strictures (though, significantly, it is in the *piyyut* that the poet most often experimented with non-classical syllabic and strophic forms.)

Above all Halevi's devotional poems are dialogic: engaging in a sometimes anguished, sometimes comforting, yet always impassioned conversation with an absent, divine interlocutor, who wears, as tradition has it, seventy faces, and is invoked in Halevi's poetry by his various names *Yehovah, Adonai, Elohim, El* and *Yah*. The divine name is identified by Halevi as the light of God's countenance which is yearned for and sought after within the recesses of one's own being: " . . . If I could only behold / his face within my heart, my eyes / would no longer seek to gaze abroad."

But it is in Halevi's compact, nuanced *reshuyot* recited in synagogue as individual prologues to prayer, that one hears the purest and most penetrating strains in the poet's wide-ranging corpus. Frequently written in the first person singular and evoking the courtly world of straying gazelles, abandoned brides, and ruined desert campsites, the poems address the questing soul, the *neshama,* or God as the *Anima Mundi,* the Divine Influence ever on the threshold between the celestial and terrestrial worlds. It is here, in a stance of apparent self-effacement and trust – recalling the medieval Islamic condition of *tawakkul,* "acceptance" – as a *shaliah tsibbur,* a precentor (the *sod neshamot,* or "fellowship/of souls flocking toward the Lord's bounty"), that Halevi's own voice – sensuous, intense, rhythmically attuned to the disquiet and longings of the self – is most acutely felt. Thus in the first of Halevi's short lyrics addressed to the fledgling soul – and remarkable for its homophonic wordplay and tight tonal braiding – the urgent whisper of conscience steadily rises in the softest of crescendos: "Asleep, face nestled in your child-hood pillow,/how long will you slumber there?/Mind this: youth is brushed off like fluff./Imagine such nascent days lasting forever./Rise, see how your white hairs rebuke you like heralds" ("Admonitions", 1). For centuries Halevi's gentle coaxing and prodding of the self toward moral recti-tude was to become synonymous with the trials and aspira-tions of a dispersed nation.

SOMETIME IN the late 1130s, pessimistic over the fate of the Jews of Sepharad, as Andalusia was called in Hebrew, and convinced that traditional Judaism was at an impasse in exile, Halevi decided to undertake a pilgrimage to Jerusalem. This in itself was not uncommon at the time. The poet, however, made it clear that he intended not simply to tour but to remain in Palestine. Friends opposed his resolve. How could he leave his family – his only daughter and Yehuda, his grandson? And why forsake the relative security of Cordoba for a hazardous sea voyage that, if survived, would bring him to a country ravaged by Crusaders? But Halevi had already declared in *The Kuzari* that full communion with God could be achieved only by living in the Holy Land. That land might be devastated, but for the poet it had once been the locus of God's "heart and eyes", and it was where the feminine aspect of the divine, the *Shekhinah*, would return if only the proper cultic rites were performed in the former holy sites.

Written in Judeo-Arabic in the form of a Socratic dialogue, *The Kuzari* offers a curious blend of poeticisms, cultic and theophanic thinking, and religious conservatism. For all its humanism and emotional immediacy, the book's essential notions of a lost, ideal past, the burden of exile, of Revelation and Election, the sacred status of the Hebrew language and of *Eretz Yisrael*, the land of Israel, suggest a form of cultural isolationism running counter to the very ideals of the Jewish Andalusian upper class. As noted, the latter had hitherto immersed itself in the sciences, in philosophy, rhetoric and the arts, and in the sensual aesthetics that characterized its Arab host culture. *The Book of Refutation and Proof with Regard to the Humiliated Religion*, as *The Kuzari* was titled in full, turned away from rational philosophy as an end in itself. Halevi, now in his late fifties or early sixties, was anxious to reinvest Judaism with the direct experience of the divine order. Reason was subordinate to the Torah: "In the service of God there is no arguing, reasoning, and debating. Had this been possible, philosophers with their wisdom and acumen would have achieved even more than Israel." Halevi – or at least the figure of the scholar who addresses the king of the Khazars and who appears to be speaking in Halevi's voice – even indicts his own poetry as he warns against "cramping Hebrew" into the meters of a foreign nation that could never equal the noble, prophetic power of ancient "oral communication". In its stead Halevi proposed a form of pietism, a social and psychic retreat that consolidated, as recent scholarship has shown,

Jewish mystical thought and Muslim neoplatonism; the latter received its fullest expression in the widespread Sufi teachings that had effectively evolved in and around Halevi's time.

The winds of discord were blowing from every direction. The poet's admonitions and self-questionings, his call to rid oneself of time's trappings, "as birds / shake off last night's dew from their feathers", and his emphasis on the immediacy of revelation ("Your nearness manifest, not in dark speeches"), spoke with unprecedented force to a people living in a precarious age, who, even as they held on to their ideals of linguistic perfectibility, of learning and material comfort, became increasingly preoccupied with theories of eschatology and the imminent arrival of the Messiah – calculations which the poet himself entertains in "Startled Awake". And yet Halevi remained, in Ross Brann's apt phrase, ever "the compunctious poet". Throughout his wanderings within Spain and beyond its frontiers, he continued to write secular poems of unrivaled ease and elegance that seem, at least on the surface, to run counter to his religious pronouncements.

The range of Halevi's writings – and there are close to a thousand poems – defies and ultimately transcends any easy categorization. Even the poet's yearning for the Holy Land which has always been perceived as quintessentially Jewish, was not unaffected by the language and figurative topoi of Muslim-Andalusian nostalgia for its own heartland in the east. So the lament over the abandoned desert abode, the archetype of Arabic literature and what Jaroslav Stetkevych has called "the bedrock of the image as remembrance", dovetails with Halevi's repeated evocation of the ruins of the deserted Holy Sanctuary. Longing will soon be replaced, moreover, by the actual journey east, a mythopoetic quest not unlike the trials and adventures of the poet-hero in the pre-Islamic *qasida*, a form taken up and adapted by the Hebrew poets of the medieval Arab world. This is not to say that Halevi's imagery and language aren't firmly embedded in Jewish history and liturgy, but rather that it is the particular confluence of traditions, Jewish and Arabic, religious and secular, that gives the poetry its driving force.

It is best then to treat with caution such received – and revered – images of Halevi as the singularly pious devotee or, alternatively, as the romantic proto-nationalist and the epitome – for the early Zionists – of the emancipated Jewish soul. Portrayed as a man of the deepest convictions, and as one admirer wrote in 1130, "the quintessence and embodiment of our country", Halevi may, in fact, have been of two minds. Andalusian culture had too strong a grip on his imagination to be simply "cast behind" as he proposes in one of his poems. How to explain, for example, Halevi's letter to his friend and business partner, Ibn Halfon, where he describes *The Kuzari* as "a trifle"? Was this mere modesty, or did it reflect some genuine unease regarding the views propounded by the scholarly figure, or *haver*, who speaks in defense of Judaism?[3] In the end, the closer one scrutinizes the life and the work, the more ambiguous and paradoxical become the figure of the poet and his attendant roles as courtier, physician, scholar, religious apologist, public emissary, moralist, reviver of the biblical Levite tradition of sacred song ("If you revive/the ancient songs and dance," Halevi writes in "Primed for Flight", "he will renew his mighty deeds, restore life/to the dead, flesh to dry bones") and solitary pilgrim.

By the time he had made his decision to leave Spain (a decision which came shortly before a second, more fanatical, wave of Berbers from North Africa, the Almohads, invaded Andalusia), Halevi was writing – and I am thinking in particular of the poet's sweeping "Zion, Won't You Ask" of "Primed for Flight" and "Can Lifeless Bodies" – more as visionary than as court poet, though the figure of the courtier was never completely discarded. It would vie to the very end with that of the repentant poet forever on the verge of abandoning the sensory appeal of Andalusian court life. One could not be content living "like a bird leashed/to a boy's hand", Halevi writes in a poem defending his decision to leave for the east, the line neatly alluding to Job 40.29: "Wilt thou play with him as with a bird? Or wilt thou bind him for thy maidens?" More than once he declares that he is going to give up the writing of poetry altogether. Poetry was like "the foam of the sea", as contrasted with wisdom, which was like the vast sea itself – an analogy that anticipates Mallarmé: "Nothing, this foam, immaculate verse." And yet soon enough the storm-tossed seas and the abyss that "hissed unappeased" would become the subject of the poet's remarkable final testimony.

IN THE SUMMER of 1140, with his son-in-law, Yitzhak Ibn Ezra (in all probability the son of the renowned biblical commentator and poet, Avraham Ibn Ezra), and a second companion, Abu l-Rabi Ibn Gabbai, Halevi embarked for Alexandria on the Sultan's ship. Sailing from the southeast coast of Spain to Alexandria took roughly six weeks. The small wooden vessels, *garibs* in Arabic, that plied the Mediterranean offered their passengers little safety or comfort. They were no more than seagoing barges, shaped like oversized nutshells and propelled by oars and stiff, square-rigged sails. Passengers, who were expected to bring their own provisions, slept on deck, pressed against bales of merchandise.

The perils of the sea were compounded by the ever-present dangers of starvation, illness and piracy. Freebooters lay in wait in their light galleys, or *ghurabs* (Arabic for "edge of sword") just off the coast of modern-day Libya. Travelers captured by pirates would either be offered for ransom (some years earlier, while living in Toledo, Halevi had been personally involved in raising money to ransom a Jewish woman), or else sold on the slave market after having been tortured and stripped of all their belongings.

Halevi's ship, at least two weeks overdue, sailed into the port of Alexandria on September 9, 1140. The poet was given a hero's welcome. Indeed, a letter written by the Alexandrian businessman Abu Nasr Ibn Avraham – one of many documents uncovered in the 1950s in the Cairo Geniza by S.D. Goitein[4] – describes in detail how Halevi was showered with invitations by the city notables. One such Alexandrian, Ibn Matruch, even used his influence with the *wali*, the superintendent of police, to have the poet invited to his home for a Friday meal.

Religious devotion and physical yearning, the fusion of the sublime and the profane, find their fullest expression in Halevi's majestic sequence written on the sea, which he must have handed over to his new friends and admirers soon after landing in Alexandria. Enveloped in the sacral language of scripture and depicting the stormy voyage, the sequence of poems may be read both for their graphic portrayal of high adventure on the sea and as an allegory of longing, repentance, and, ultimately, deliverance:

> Leviathan
> whitens the surf with age in its churning.
> Drenched in spray, the ship's
> snatched by the hands of the thieving sea.
> Waters rage, but I stand firm,
> my spirits raised, Lord,
> drawing near to your sanctuary.

What intrigues in this last chapter of Halevi's life, however, is not only the poet's hazardous sea-voyage, but his prolonged, socially gratifying stay in Egypt. Halevi's professed desire was to get to the Holy Land as soon as possible. "I hoped to make of Alexandria a short cut," he writes in rhymed prose to the *Nagid* Shmuel ben Hananya, head of the Jewish community of Cairo. And yet Halevi remained in Egypt for nine months, spending long, leisurely hours in the home of Aharon Ibn al-Ammani, the chief judge, or *dayyan*, of the Jewish community in Alexandria, and, like Halevi, a poet and a physician. His home, with its luxurious gardens, fountains and pools, is described in a series of dedicatory poems Halevi wrote during his sojourn in Egypt. Published by al-Ammani while the poet was away in Cairo between December and March, they caused something of a stir: how could the esteemed poet, the "sweet singer of Zion", now in his sixties and ostensibly on a pilgrimage, compose not only improvisations on the gift of a chicken or, on another occasion, a razor blade, but also, and in particular, poems of sensual, even erotic appeal?

Halevi's poems written in Egypt recall the poetry of his youth, though again, the public and the private figure of the poet, the devotional and the profane, cannot be readily separated. "In Alexandria" offers a dizzying evocation of landscapes both real and imagined, where practically every line is poised between the concrete, natural image and the distant past of the Bible. A reader well-versed in scriptures would identify the first line as coming from Ezekiel: "Then all the princes of the sea shall come down from their thrones, and lay away their robes, and strip-off their richly woven garments; they shall clothe themselves with trembling." But it is Halevi's recalling of his own childhood innocence, and his eroticized sensory reawakening, that charges the poem with a sense of unexpected immediacy:

> Has time taken off its clothes of trembling
> and decked itself out in riches,
> and has the earth put on fine-spun linen
> and set its beds in gold brocade?
> All the fields of the Nile are checkered,
> as though the bloom of Goshen
> were woven straps of a breastplate,
> and lush oases dark-hued yarn,
> and Raamses and Pithom laminated goldleaf.
>   Girls on the riverbank, a bevy of fawns,
> linger, their wrists heavy with bangles—
> anklets clipping their gait.
>   The heart enticed
> forgets its age, remembers boys or girls

in the garden of Eden, in Egypt, along the Pishon,
running on the green to the river's edge;
the wheat is emerald tinged with red,
and robed in needlework;
it sways to the whim of the sea breeze,
as though bowing in thanks to the Lord . . .

And so Halevi tarried in Egypt. At one point the poet got himself into a potentially dangerous situation when he tried to persuade a convert to Islam named Ibn Basri to travel with him to the Holy Land and there re-embrace Judaism. Ibn Basri apparently not only refused but also reported Halevi to the authorities. The poet soon found himself forced to justify his actions in front of the secret police, the governor, and finally the judge of Alexandria. Had it not been for Halevi's renown and high position, concludes Abu Nasr Ibn Avraham, in yet another letter recovered from the Cairo Geniza, his life would certainly have been threatened by the angry mob that instead directed its ire against the hapless apostate.

A revealing letter by Halevi – the fifth to be found written in the poet's own hand – composed in Judeo-Arabic shortly after the poet landed in Alexandria and addressed to his close friend Halfon Ibn Natanel, surfaced only in 1998. Retrieved by the Geniza scholars Ezra Fleischer and Moshe Gil, it reads:

> And the people had fine manners and extraordinarily courteous demeanors and speeches and praise and refreshments, in a quantity that embarrassed me. And outwardly I participated in all this . . . [but] within [these things] weighed heavily upon me. For I do not believe at all in all these things, and I had wanted quite the opposite of this, that is, to go apart and be alone, for I am almost one who is expecting death at any moment. But for the benefit a man derives from those he meets – it is impossible not to accept the expressions of graciousness and the benevolent demeanor towards me.

Did Halevi travel to Cairo not merely for pleasure, at the invitation of the city's *dayyan*, but in search of an alternative, overland route to Palestine, via Sinai and Gaza, as the contemporary scholar Joseph Yahalom has suggested? Or was the prolongation of his stay in Egypt in some way connected to his relationship with his son-in-law, a poet of exceptional talent, who refused to accompany Halevi on the final leg of his voyage to the Holy Land, and who eventually settled in Baghdad and converted to Islam? Then again, Egypt's religious significance cannot be underestimated: as the locus of the Exodus, and of countless miracles (". . . tread lightly, / don't step boldly, / / down streets where the Matronita passed / seeking the blood-pact on doorposts"), Egypt was indeed holy ground, a vast arena where the great dramatic moments of early Jewish history were enacted. In kabbalistic literature, the land of bondage and freedom was even perceived as a symbolic birth canal, a sacred passageway to Zion. A nine-month period of gestation may have been for Halevi precisely the time needed before finally making his entry into the Holy Land. In one of his sea poems the poet is quite explicit in his depiction of the voyage as a prolonged and painful delivery: "Though anguished, like a woman / in labor – panting, unable / to push her firstborn out –/ and though lacking food and drink, / the sweetness of your name / is all my nourishment."

Whatever the case, the Mediterranean was simply too dangerous to navigate during the winter months. Captains of merchant vessels, even those sailing the estimated ten-day voyage from Alexandria to Ashkelon (then in Fatimid hands) or Acre (controlled by the Crusaders) along the Syro-Palestinian coast, dared not undertake such a journey until "the time of the opening of the seas" in late spring.

Yehuda Halevi boarded a ship for Palestine on May 7. It was still in port, however, on the eleventh. Abu Nasr writes to Halfon Ibn Natanel: "All the ships going to Spain, al-Mahdiya [southern Tunisia], Tripoli, Sicily and Byzantium have departed and have encountered a propitious wind. However, the ship of the ruler of al-Mahdiya has not yet moved. Our master Yehuda Halevi boarded it four days ago, but the wind is not favorable for them. May God grant them safety."

Of the nine poems written at sea, two are addressed to the west wind. "Your Breeze, Western Shore" entreats the west wind to subdue the east wind that was preventing the ship from sailing to the Holy Land. And in "Break not, Lord, the breakers of the sea . . .", the poet expresses his gratitude to the west wind for filling the sails of the ship. It is possible, and so S.D. Goitein has argued, that these two poems were written not on the high seas, but aboard ship just outside the port of Alexandria, while Halevi waited for the weather to clear, and before meeting for the last time with Abu Nasr to whom the poems would have been entrusted. If so, they – and, possibly, "Stop the surging of the sea . . ." – are the last extant poems to come from Halevi's pen. The short lyric of thanksgiving – which, for formal reasons (and in keeping with Heinrich Brody's *diwan* of Halevi's poems), I have placed at the helm of the sequence – would have been composed in the sudden surge of excitement as the west wind finally filled the ship's sails.

That would have been on May 14, the first day of Shavuot, the Feast of Weeks. On his return from bidding farewell to Halevi, Abu Nasr writes in haste: "The west wind has risen, the ship has sailed."

In October and November of that year, the poet's demise in July is lamented in two separate letters written by friends of Halevi's in Egypt. In one, we learn that Halevi's grandson, Yehuda Ibn Ezra, was intending to join the poet – perhaps with his mother – in the Holy Land, and that Halevi had handed over to Abu Nasr his own turban and coat, specifying that he was to pass the turban to "the boy" if he arrived in Alexandria within the year.

The location and the circumstances surrounding the poet's death have remained open to conjecture. Did his ship founder? Was it captured and plundered by pirates? Then again, perhaps he did finally reach the shores of a land that had haunted and pressed upon his imagination for so many years. Legend insists that a Saracen horseman trampled Halevi to death as the poet recited his stately "Zion, Won't You Ask" in front of the gates of Jerusalem. A highly improbable story, as Jerusalem at the time was part of the Latin Kingdom, and Christians, not Muslims, ruled the city. Heinrich Heine, however, whose imagination was not untouched by the romantic orientalizing of his times, drew on the same legend in describing the poet's ill-fated yet heroic end in his *Hebrew Melodies*, where he would also declare that "When God fashioned Halevi's soul, he was so delighted with his handiwork that he kissed it, and the music of that kiss echoes through all the songs of our consecrated poet." A more likely ending, suggested by the Israeli historian Elchanan Reiner, is that Halevi landed in the seaport of Acre, known at the time as a point of departure for pilgrims, and then traveled due east, to the ancient city of Tiberias on the shores of the Sea of Galilee, home for centuries to a Jewish community of scholars and mystics.[4] Might he have then traveled to Jerusalem, the locus of his yearning and "the foundation /of all foundations", for a brief visit – or rather circumambulation – of the holy sites? Staying in Jerusalem for any length of time was out of the question, as the Jewish and Muslim communities of the city had been brought to ruin by the Crusaders. Halevi, if he did indeed reach Jerusalem, would have had to retrace his steps to Tiberias. It was there, Reiner claims, that he died – and may still be buried – thus bringing to a close a life marked by partings, yet survived by the gift of song.

GABRIEL LEVIN

1. In speaking of Halevi's early biography I have followed Haim Schirmann's chronology as presented in his magisterial *The History of Hebrew Poetry in Muslim Spain* [Hebrew], Edited, Supplemented and Annotated by Ezra Fleischer (Jerusalem: The Magnes Press, 1995). Halevi's date of birth has never been ascertained. Schirmann gives it as before 1075. However, it should be noted that in recent years Joseph Yahalom has argued in favor of returning to the opinion held by Halevi's first modern editors, Samuel Luzzatto and Heinrich Brody, namely that Halevi was born in the border town of Toledo – rather than Tudela – *after*, and not before 1075. Toledo, not unlike the smaller, more remote Tudela, was a Muslim town with a mixed population of Arabs, Jews, Christians, Slavs and *muwallads* (converts to Islam), which would soon fall under Christian rule. Moshe Ibn Ezra writes in his treatise on poetry *The Book of Conversation and Discussion* that Halevi was a "son [resident] of Toledo and afterwards a son of Cordoba", which still leaves one guessing. Tudela, on the other hand, may have appeared as a backwater town, but it produced in Halevi's lifetime two other remarkable Jewish figures: the poet and biblical commentator Avraham Ibn Ezra, and Benjamin of Tudela who famously chronicled his travels in the Near East. Growing up under Muslim and Hebrew tutelage in a multilingual frontier town might help us understand the complex, antithetical components of Halevi's identity, it might also explain the poet's literary finesse and mastery at an early age of Hebrew and classical Arabic sources, even though in his correspondence and poetry he complains of having been raised in *Seir*, or Christian Spain, which was considered far less civilized than the south.

Yahalom, moreover, has suggested that Halevi never met Moshe Ibn Ezra in Granada, but rather befriended the poet in the north, sometime in the 1090s, after the latter poet had fled Andalusia. It was only subsequent to their meeting, according to Yahalom, that Halevi traveled south to Granada where he may have remained for a short period before moving back to Toledo.

Halevi's epistle in rhymed prose addressed to Moshe Ibn Ezra appears, along with a number of other epistles written while in Andalusia, in Halevi's *diwan* compiled by his twelfth-century redactor, Hiyya ben Yitzhak.

2. Arabic quantitative meters were first adapted into Hebrew by Dunash Ibn Labrat (died c. 990), who was born in Baghdad and lived in North Africa before moving to Andalusia and serving in the Cordovan court of Hasday Ibn Shaprut, the Jewish vizier of Abd al-Rahman III. Each line, called a *beit*, "house", and generally

monorhymed, was divided into equal halves – *delet*, "door", and *soger*, "lock" – which were further subdivided into regular patterns of short and long syllables, called *ammudim*, "columns" (the equivalent of the English "foot"). Such terminology is not without significance when one considers the heightened sensitivity to ornamental architecture in Andalusia and its conscious manipulation of surface and depth, stasis and movement. Although the craft of poetry was often compared to the jeweler's art, the poem itself was a house of many rooms.

3. In another letter to Halfon, written after *The Kuzari* and shortly before leaving for the East, Halevi enclosed a Judeo-Arabic treatise on Hebrew meters that poignantly embodies the poet's cultural ambivalence. Halevi's opening and closing statements roundly denounce the use of Arabizing Hebrew prosody, even as he proceeds to illustrate its applicability in twelve succinct epigrams, illustrative of varying quantitative metrical patterns, which lament his friend's eminent departure for Egypt. See Ross Brann, *The Compunctious Poet: Cultural Ambiguity and Hebrew Poetry in Muslim Spain* (Baltimore: Johns Hopkins University Press, 1991), pp. 89–118. Halevi's debt to Arab-Andalusian culture is discussed as well in Ammiel Alcalay, *After Jews and Arabs: Remaking Levantine Culture* (Minneapolis: University of Minneapolis Press, 1993), pp. 173–5. For Halevi's poetics of longing and deferral see Sidra DeKoven Ezrahi, *Booking Passage: Exile and Homecoming in the Modern Jewish Imagination* (Berkeley: University of California Press, 2000), pp. 33–51.

4. In 1896 two Englishwomen climbed up to the storeroom of the ancient Ben Ezra synagogue in Old Cairo and found, to their astonishment, a huge scrap-heap of tattered writings in Hebrew characters: epistles, marriage contracts, business inventories, collections of poems, fragments of prayerbooks, responsa to Jewish law, court records, which had been preserved for centuries, in accordance with the rabbinic injunction against desecrating the Holy Tongue. That same year Solomon Schechter of Cambridge University sailed to Egypt and gained permission to haul back to England over forty thousand fragments from the Geniza, now forming the Taylor-Schechter collection in Cambridge. News of Schechter's expedition to Cairo brought a host of scholars, private collectors and dealers to Old Cairo in the hope of purchasing documents from the Ben Ezra Geniza, and by the early twentieth century Geniza fragments were scattered among two dozen different libraries around the world.

Shlomo Dov Goitein pioneered Geniza scholarship in the twentieth century. Garnering the particulars of everyday life documented in the Geniza, he reconstructed the social and cultural fabric of the oriental Jewish communities during the Middle Ages. Cairo, it should be noted, had become by the twelfth century the political, commercial and cultural center of Jewry in the east and its highly cosmopolitan nature is reflected in the variety of Geniza documents, ingathered from the furthest reaches of the Muslim world. Letters uncovered in the Geniza dealing with the late biography of Halevi, and in particular with his voyage to and stay in Egypt, appear in S.D. Goitein, *A Mediterranean Society: The Jewish Communities of the Arab World as Portrayed in the Documents of the Cairo Genizah*, vol. 5 (Berkeley: University of California Press, 1988). See also S.D. Goitein, "The Biography of Rabbi Judah Ha-Levi in the Light of the Cairo Geniza Documents", *Proceedings of the American Academy for Jewish Research*, vol. 28 (New York: 1959), pp. 41–56. Full documentation of letters to, from and about Halevi appears in Moshe Gil and Ezra Fleischer, *Yehuda Ha-Levi and His Circle: 55 Geniza Documents* [Hebrew] (Jerusalem: World Union of Jewish Studies, 2001). In addition to two complete *diwans*, there exist over a thousand Cairo Geniza fragments of Yehuda Halevi's poetry, which attest to the immense popularity of his work in the twelfth and thirteenth centuries not only in Egypt but also beyond its immediate borders.

5. Tiberias had played a crucial role for the Jews of Galilee in Byzantine and Muslim Palestine, a position which only grew after the Crusader conquest of Jerusalem in 1099 and the dispersion of its Jewish community. Elchanan Reiner has written of the centrality of the Galilee as a locus of eschatological belief, pilgrimage and burial [see "From Joshua to Jesus: The Transformation of a Biblical Story to a Local Myth: A Chapter in the Religious Life of the Galilean Jew", in *Sharing the Sacred: Religious Contacts and Conflicts in the Holy Land*, edited by A. Kofsky and G. Stroumsa (Jerusalem: Yad Ben Zvi, 1998)]. The religious importance of Tiberias is further attested by the fact that at the beginning of the thirteenth century the body of Maimonides, the most renowned Jewish religious figure of the medieval world, was brought from Cairo to Palestine to be buried in Tiberias, and not in Jerusalem, and it appears that his son and grandson were also buried in the same family plot. Halevi's fellow Tudelean, Benjamin of Tudela, who arrived in Palestine twenty years after the poet's demise, mentions in his *Travels* visiting the graves of illustrious Jews in Tiberias. Among the names listed is that of Yehuda Halevi. A footnote to the text, however, emends the name as Yonatan Ben Levi (a minor Talmudic sage), consequently leaving unclear Benjamin's original designation.

Poems from the Diwan

A Sleepless Night

A sleepless night in which the hours hang heavy.
  Friends leave tomorrow. Night, lead on softly
and spread your raven wings over dawn's first rays.
  My tears, raining down on their carriage,
delay their journey; a cloud, raised by my sulking heart,
  veils the break of day from their sight.
If only my sighs would turn to smoke and blaze
  into a scorching fire, hampering their departure
from my tent, at least until I give my consent.

Cheated

1

Parting from my fawn has made me vile
    and wretched, my body's a shadow
        grown old, and not by dint of years –
to this the fleeting days of my life
    attest. Cheated, I've aged.
        Should he return, I'll swiftly regain my youth.

2

Hills, mountains, bear greetings
    primed with tears, to eyes
        shadowed with the soot of my pupils
and fingertips stained in my heart's blood.
    Though I stir not her love, tears
        will rouse her pity.

A Reminder

The breeze wings my greetings
toward you
>   friend,

lifting the mid-day heat;

all I ask: never to forget
the day we swore

>   a love pact

and parted,

under the apple tree.

To Shlomo Ibn al-Muallim

Easy, my firm-hearted, tender-hipped one,
   gently now, as I bow before you.
My eyes alone are ravished by your sight.
   Surely my intentions are pure, but not my eyes.
Let them gather from your features
   roses and lilies sown together.
I'll rake your cheeks' embers, quenching fire
   with fire, and when thirsty find
water there. I'll suck your coal-hot lips,
   my jaws like tongs – for life
hangs between their scarlet threads,
   and my death is twilit.
Rows of flowing myrrh richly embroidered
   resemble dusklight at noon;
even Bezalel couldn't have stitched so well
   and might have asked Shlomo to lend a hand.
The hands that adorned the parchment surpass
   in skill those which rouged the gazelle's face.
Such writing threads pearls on a necklace
   and furtively kindles Egyptian enchantments.
He who has seized the wings of love
   seizes hearts and is seized by all hands.
I said: my joy and beloved is mine
   and love hasn't wrung me dry.
On a heavenly cherub I'll wander far off,
   though friends are my surety, not my feet
that pursue a far-reaching angel who's ascended
   a swift cloud and lightning fills his hands . . .

Wake Up from Your Slumber

Wake up from your slumber, friend –
    I'd rest satisfied
        by your waking figure.

If in your sleep you behold someone
    kissing your lips, know
        it is I, your dream's diviner.

Graceful Doe, Pity This Heart

Graceful doe, pity this heart where you've dwelled.
    Know the day you leave I'll fall apart.
Even now, as my eyes confront your splendor,
    I'm stung by your cheeks' vipers
    whose venom burns and drives me away.

Her firm breasts have plundered my heart.
    A stone heart that bears two apples
set side by side like lances. Their fire
    inflames my heart – though they won't come near,
    they sap my vigor, and feel no shame.

This gazelle defies God's laws with her eyes.
    Her malice is lethal, won't be appeased.
Have you ever seen a lion's heart and doe-eyed lids
    that prey like a lioness? Their honed
    arrows quaff my blood. They want me dead.

Once I reeled from the wine of her love.
    Couriers she'd dispatched bearing greetings
and entreaties were pried for news as soon
    as they returned: "Sweet envoys, tell me more!"
    Seduced by such tidings my spirits revived.

Grazing one day in her garden I fondled
    her breasts. "Remove," she said, "those clumsy
hands of yours." Her smooth words melted my heart.
    These breasts, dear, are extra tender – I'm through
    with your games. You men are all the same.

A Small Consolation

Lovely doe, I'm hostage to your splendor
    and labor in captivity.
Ever since parting came between us
    I've found no one that can bear comparison
to your beauty.
          So I take comfort in an apple,
    fragrant as the ornament of your breath,
shapely as your breasts, its sheen
    as the sheen of carnelian on your cheeks.

Elegy for a Child

Child snatched from the arms of his begetter.
   Deprived, he recoils in grief
to say, perish the day I was born
   if only I hadn't seen the rust
      of this world, the death of a child.

How suddenly, all of a sudden, bereaved
   of the child I nourished and raised —
I've laid my glory in the dust,
   my splendor defiled,
he who filled me with hope the day I boasted
   unknowing what day would father.

Pity me, oh pity me, friends,
   for the Lord has wrested from my arms
the light of my eyes, a child fondled
   and now cleansed in the waters of my tears
and buried between my ribs
   as I speak of him at every moment,
my heart, my heart, how it aches!
   My heart that has died with the child.

In Praise of Shlomo Ibn Ghiyyat

A generous eye roams as a merchant,
taking sleeplessness and giving pearls and onyx –
crystal drops whose beads, if not for their scalding grief,
would string together like a necklace –
it wanders softly weeping over the ruins of the lover's
    dwelling
neither hearing nor speaking a word.
The hand of parting that scattered their encampment
razes the walls of my heart.
How strange, as if I'd never set eyes on the place,
though heart intuits what my eyes estrange.
Before the Lord is the wanderer's path – bearing sleep
of a bountiful eye that squanders its riches.
I might find comfort in the departure of troop upon
    troop –
if the constellations but sparked a reminder:
now the moon binds the queen, believing
it has shifted and sunk like lead into the western sea,
brandishing a flaming sword of lightning
it rebukes the back of the earth with bolts of fire
that swirl and rebound – a young girl
whose skirt-fringe sparkles, billowing in wind.
Earth looms darkly armored, and stars
pitch smoldering firebrands;
the moon dims as it speeds forward, then holds
course in the heavens, resembling a gold
clasp in a mantle; its face, illumined in the dust
of battle, is the face of a princess urging her warriors on;
a flock shivers, then hunkers down, as though
none but the sick and defeated were left.
I weep for the leave-taking of the daughters of the Great
    Bear,
and envy the Pleiades for being fixed forever.

Does it grip the skies to keep it from tilting,
or measure the span of the heavenly spheres?
Have the chariots of the sun pulled to a halt, are the
      bolted
gates of the east winds blocking its path?
Can mother of pearl turn emerald, and will dawn's
blush from behind dark locks ever dawn?
How tired I grow of night, the moon seems to me
washed in ebony and blotched with the plague.
Whenever I discern a moving tongue of fire I rejoice –
hoping for the slightest sign of daybreak dawning.
Can night dark as an Ethiopian ever change its skin,
or the celestial leopard miss its spots?
The eye bleakly scans the skies for a ray of sun,
the bells of its chariot late in ringing.

A gentle breeze spying in the furrowed beds
detects love in the heart of the myrtle
as birds trill on the wing, and the distant
dove stammers – though to me she speaks clearly.
She distils charm and pours lovers' dew like manna,
shaking from her feathers last night's drops.
Does the incense she burns rise from a bundle of myrrh,
or is it Shlomo's song tied to her wing?
Dawn glows from behind black rows,
joined as darkness and the morning-watch are linked:
its ranks are night, its message daybreak,
like a girl's tresses concealing her cheeks.
A song – that swears it was carved
from mountains of myrrh, not from resin,
row upon row like the tents of Kedar, and sheets
of paper like Solomon's curtains, *swart and beautiful.*
No human eye has ever seen such rows set in stones of fire
until it beholds his song in the letter.
How can his words not spark off a blaze,
as fire to the chest, or flame to tow?

His every word is sealed in my heart,
each letter inscribed within for safe-keeping,
a flowerbed woven by the hand of fancy
whose grace encircles and is set as a wreath –
choicest of fruits and the prize of songs whets the palate,
my tongue sings of the daughters of the vine.

Here is the fruit of song from your friend
yielding its harvest every month, though love ripens
    continually –
he's come as the best of times draws to an end
and can only stare into the past.
He is one of the invited – and though his name is
    unrecorded
tradition proudly amends his lateness.
He chases after the noble, clings to their counsel,
they are the lion – and he the tail.
People sleep until dawn wakes them –
yet his soul's awake and stirs the heart of dawn
to attend to his friend's devotion
and refine his love for him from inside-out.
Take from the slow of speech a clear language, cast in
    gold,
and set like links in the poem's weave –
the daughter of friendship carved from love's mountain
hastens to purchase your affection.
Dawn breeze, search out the face of all true lovers
and speak untiringly of Shlomo's welfare.

After Mutanabbi

The day I sat him on my knee, he gazed
at his own image in my pupils, then kissed each eye
    in play –
or rather his reflection embraced, not my eyes.

Three Bridal Songs

1

A canopy shields the precious pair
    exuding sweet scented
myrrh. "I'm host
    to sun and moon,"
it boasts on the day of the harvest
    and screens the guests from the sun's glare
lest they burn.
               Friends,
see how all is well
    and drink to your heart's content
in the pavilion's shade
    from where the sun is glimpsed.

2

Young fawns stood among the myrtle
    and sent forth liquid myrrh
to the very ends of the earth.
    Coveting the pungency of their aroma,
the myrtle spread its wings like an angel,
    as if to cover the scent
with its own, but instead found itself
    overpowered by their fragrance.

3

You are a flowering myrtle among the trees
  of Eden, a shining Orion
among the constellations.

God has given you a bundle
  of myrrh made with his own hands,
not the perfumer's.

A dove nests in the myrtle
  that has stolen her fragrance,
its branches soaked in her balm.

When you're with her don't go looking
  for the sun, just as when she's in your arms
she needn't look for the moon.

The Fawn

Such a stunning fawn with a lion's roar
  never was nor will there ever be.
He thunders and preys like a young lion and yet
  kissing his prey's mouth life restores.
His shapely figure, and not his bellow
  melts the heart of the lion-hearted.
My spirit is in his hands, at his word
  I'd die, while friends sigh, "Where is he?"

To Yitzhak the Orphan (Ibn Elitom)

Only yesterday earth suckled the autumn rain
like an infant, the clouds its nurse,
or else it was a bride sequestered in winter,
her soul longing for the season of love.
She yearns for courting-time until summer
comes and the heart is healed.
Robed in gold brocade and fine linen
like a girl who delights to pamper herself,
each day she slips on a new gown
before handing it over to the close at hand –
from day to day she renews
the color of plants: ruby, emerald, pearl;
she pales, turns green, blushes,
like a gazelle approaching her lover.
Her flowers are so radiant I imagined
she'd plundered the heavenly bodies.
At dawn we entered the grove of her gifts,
must of the vine fanning the flames of love
cold as the cold of snow in the hand,
though raging like fire in the entrails.
Out of the earthenware it rises like the sun:
fetch a crystal glass, fill it to the brim,
and we'll walk in the shade of her garden
that laughs even as the clouds weep,
it rejoices as tears streak down its face
(pearls scattered from a necklace)
thrills to the swallow's song, as if it were wine,
while doves cooing in sweet counsel
hidden in the foliage, resemble a songstress
who sings and swirls behind a screen.

I seek out the early morning breeze
laced with the fragrance of my friend,

the wind teases the myrtle, whose balm
extends to distant lovers, its branches
spring up, then bend, even as palm fronds clap
at choiring birds, they sway and bow
before Yitzhak, his name sending ripples
of laughter across the face of the earth.
She says: 'Hasn't God given me good reason to laugh
since I hold tight Yitzhak's cords?'
I say: No one denies my words when I pay homage
to his honor, every ear approves.
The fame of the noble cuts across good
and evil, but his name without question
is entirely good. How pleasant to hear him
approaching, even as my mind dwells on his memory —
but upon seeing him I double
my praise and repeat my song.
It is for you, noble Yitzhak, my tongue
grows eloquent and won't cease to compose —
in the lifelong pact we struck
I swore never to stop singing your praises.
How then begin to extol you
since your soul cleaves to all that is precious?
Generosity has pitched its tent within you,
and reason camps at your doorstep.
Your soul, slaked by the fountain of knowledge,
has delved into the mystery of last things,
she has built her nest in your heart
where she snuggles in play.
So be fruitful and multiply, and pass to your seed
your generous spirit and liberal hand,
and you will behold your children's offspring,
and the skies will shower them with mercy.

Ophra Washes Her Clothes

Ophra washes her clothes
   in the stream
      of tears
   I've shed,

she spreads them out in the sun
   of her splendor –
      she doesn't
   need the creek

when she has my eyes,
   nor any sun
      other than
   her beauty's warmth.

Why Sweetheart Keep Your Envoys

Why sweetheart keep your envoys
    from the lover whose flesh aches
with your pain? Know he thinks nothing
    of time unless he hears the voice
of your greeting, but if we're doomed to part,
    stand still a moment as I gaze
at your face. Has my heart stopped in its ribcage
    or wandered off on your trail?
For love's sake, remember your days of desire
    as I relive your carnal nights,
and as your image steals through my dreams
    let mine move through yours.
Between us surge waves of a sea
    of tears that keep me from reaching you,
yet should your steps draw near
    its waters would part before your feet.

If only I might hear after my death
    the sound of golden bells on the hem
of your skirt. Inquire of your lover's well being
    and I from the pit will ask of your love
and welfare. Your cheeks and lips
    have witnessed the shedding of my heart's blood –
will you deny it when they testify
    to the blood your hands have shed?
Why wish me dead when all I desire
    is to add more years to the years of your life;
rob me of sleep the night of my passion
    and I'll offer your lids my eye's slumber;
pools of tears are licked by your flames,
    stone hearts worn thin by your tears.
I've come to longing's fire and the waters
    of weeping, ah heart, mid tears

and embers, the bitter and sweet –
 the gall of parting, your honeyed kisses.
Your words have pounded my heart into tinsel
 and torn it to shreds in your hands.

I see the likeness of rubies over pearl
 when I behold your lips parting,
and night dims your sunlit face as you sweep
 the shock of your hair over its radiance.
Silk embroideries grace your body
 but beauty and charm shadow your eyes;
a girl's wardrobe is fashioned by human hands
 while you slip on sweetness itself, and splendor.
Sun and moon, Plough and Pleiads vie
 with each other to be your brothers and sisters;
men and women imagine they are free
 to be your slave, your handmaid.
As for me, I ask but for the thread of your lips,
 the cord wound round your hips;
my honey on your tongue, your breasts
 redolent with my spikenard and myrrh;
I've set you on my right arm as a signet,
 if only I too might be a seal on your arm.

Let my right hand forget my left,
 my doe, if I forget the love of your bridal vows.
Parting sours my heart as I remember
 the wild nectar of your kisses.
I'll drown myself in your pure myrrh,
 and water your mouth with my fragrance,
for the glory of women is in their praise, but you –
 your praises draw from you glory.
In the fields of the daughters of desire, sheaves
 of love bow to your sheaf.
Might I live to gather the myrrh and spices
 from under the tread of your feet,

though I can't hear your voice I hear
in my heart's recess the sound of your steps.
The day you revive the victims slain
by their desire for you – the day your dead
live – bid my soul return to its body,
for when you left, my soul set out after you.
For your lover's sake, lovely doe, ask
whether time will advance your petition.
Return, and our Rock will lead you back
to native ground, the haven of your desire.

Bear Arms Against the Victim

Bear arms against the victim of your desire
    and kindle love with the flame of wandering,
since you despise me, aim your lance,
    and as I loathe myself – pierce me through.
                     Fawn's companion,
it isn't fair to hold your lover captive –
    come close and the wandering chariots draw away.
Turn my sickbed into a bed of pleasure –
    and feed your lover honey and milk.

On Parting from his Friend Moshe Ibn Ezra

Even as youngsters we were marked by partings.
    The river of weeping flows through the ages,
so why quarrel with time that hasn't sinned,
    or days that bear no wrong, fixed
in their heavenly circuits where nothing is bent or twisted.
    Is this news, when nothing on earth is new,
its laws God's finger inscribed?
    How can its rules change, when the least clause
is sealed by the signet on the right hand
    supreme? Every cause chases its tail,
whatever seems novel has been here before,
    man unites only to part
and bring forth from one people a multitude –
    had mankind not dispersed,
earth wouldn't be checkered with nations.

The same potion may help or hamper,
    now it soothes, and now eats at the bone.
One man curses the day in his wrath
    and fumes at his own exasperation;
yet that very same day others bless
    and spend without a care in the world.
Food is honey in the mouth of the healthy,
    but the sick may as well chew straw.
Light dims in the eyes of the anxious, vision blurs,
    as when my own eyes grew cloudy
then gushed tears seeing Moshe go –
    fount of wisdom, in whose mouth I found
a vein of purest ore. Friendship bound us
    while the chariots of parting stood unharnessed
and I knew nothing of the shock of separation.

Though time appeared in our favor
    the daughters of fate have wrenched us apart
(we whom the daughter of love bore as twins).
    We were reared in a spice garden,
and nourished by cool draughts of wine.
    I remember you on the sundered peaks
which only yesterday seemed to you mountains of spice.
    Now my bloodshot eyes mist over
as I recall the days we shared
    that came and went like a dream.
In your place fate has put schemers
    who war in their hearts and woo with their mouths.
I try to speak to them, but instead of your manna
    their words stink of garlic and hay.
I rage at all these dolts who put on worldly airs,
    and call their pack of lies truth, and
my faith nonsense. They sow smugly and rejoice
    reaping their wheat, though blighted.

Wisdom's husk is a shell concealing precious pearls,
    but I've a lamp to rummage within
and extract its gems from hiding.
    And I won't rest until the sheaves
bow down sagely to my sheaf.
    "What good is a gold ring on a swine's snout?"
I answer the fool seeking my counsel.
    Why should I entreat the clouds to unleash
their rains on a field without seed?
    The little I ask of fortune resembles
the soul's need for living matter,
    its life support, but when the body is spent
the soul abandons its frame like an effigy.

Coda

Will I ever be the same in your absence?
    Wander and my heart wanders after you.
The day you took to the road was such a blow,
    I'd have perished if friends hadn't sworn
you'd soon return. Look how the peaks
    bear witness to a grudging sky, even now
as I weep a torrent of tears. Beacon of the west,
    come back to al-Andalus, set your seal
on every heart and hand. Pure of speech –
    how will you manage among the tongue-tied?
Can the dew of Hermon pearl the Gilboa?

Wine Songs

1

For you I'll rouse my songs day after day
    and to the pungent juice my lips taste,
"Brother," I call out to the wine-jar you've sent,
    as from its mouth I sip the essence
of its fruit, until my friends, seeing me flushed
    plead: "Haven't you had enough?"
And I: "The Gilead balm before me, how
    can I not drink to cure my ills,
and how refuse another glass when I haven't
    even reached the age of twenty-four!"

2

"Hurry now to your friend's house and his wine,
    as drinks go round like the sun
to his right. The wineglass purifies
    the wine's ruddiness – even rubies
are put to shame by its coral glow.
    It beholds and keeps secret the splendor of its vintage
until it can no longer conceal it."
    But wine imbibed banishes all my troubles;
this is the sign of the covenant
    drawn up between us – while a colorful band
of singers and musicians press round me,
    each more striking than the other.

The Night My Doe

The night my doe revealed to me
    flushed cheeks and the locks of her hair
        veiling a cool crystal brow –
the likeness of her form resembled
    the rising sun as it streaks the dawn clouds
        red with its radiant torch.

To Shlomo Ibn Feruziel upon Returning from Aragon

"An enchantress, prolonging her wanderings,
    cuts short the life of her friends:
graceful as the sun that won't turn in
    at dusk, her cheeks a flowerbed
whose fragrance never fades, slim,
    tender fleshed, beltless, except for the band
girding her narrow waist. The brightness
    of her cheeks eclipse the moon
glimpsed through her veil. She peels off
    her clothes, yet isn't naked,
for charm, splendor and beauty adorn her.
    Greetings, beauty's daughter,
from an admirer. Accept this homage,
    noble lady, from one of your slaves.
I'd sell my soul for a single night
    in which you'd free
your captive. Suffice to gaze
    and imagine all her charms:
to drink and suck her moist lips
    is my nectar – while the brim
of the cup are her fruits."

    And so she parted crimson lips
to croon, clasping her lute,
    like a mother doting on her child
who mimics the sounds formed
    in her mouth. She sang of parting,
her voice bitterly beseeching – on the verge
    of breaking into sobs.
My eyes watered seeing her pendant
    tears glittering like treasured pearls.

Why does the gazelle cry so,
     as though noble Shlomo had wandered
and left her? The minister
     whose post fit like a glove,
and who ran his affairs of state
     with a free hand. Gone –
the city dims in his wake,
     as it would brighten upon his return.
The earth appeared to rise
     wherever he set foot
till it seemed the heavens
     themselves cushioned his walk.
The land is bewildered like a lovesick
     girl whose passions are quelled
only in questing: devastated by his departure,
     her sorrows are dispelled
the moment she catches sight
     of the pleasant form of his figure returning.
Come back, Shlomo my prince, rise
     and descend from your chariot –
are not the constellations your steeds!
     Time has worn the glory
of the leaders of your generation like a robe,
     yet they are its hem,
while you are the crown jewel.

Riddles

1

What's pointed, lean, pliant
and mute – but speaking out kills
man without a sound, the blood
of idols running from its mouth?

2

What's blind, one eyed,
at everyone's beck and call –
stark naked, it spends
its life dressing others up?

3

There's no limit to what it can hold.
Small enough to grasp in your hand,
and yet you can't seize what's in it
unless you look each other in the eye.

Impromptu

Looking into the mirror I spotted
    a single strand of gray hair
and plucked it out. "I'm easy game alone,"
    it said, "but what do you plan
to do with my troops close behind me?"

The Sons of Fortune

The sons of fortune consigned to me dreams
and consolations tightly shut and sealed,
and I've nothing to grasp of such times
but an ailing heart and rot in the bones.
I've gazed at spikes of abundant wheat
but mine are spindly and blasted
and I'm left alone without companions,
brother to sorrow, friend to trouble,
my only comfort and delight's seedlings,
is seeing my brother's pleasing letters.
So-called friends drag me down from great heights
while his words pull me up from the abyss.
So why does he tarry in spite of his promises?
Why hang fire in sending me greetings?
Your welfare, and neither silver nor gold,
your letter, neither crystal nor coral –
what more have I to ask from life,
will a man draw breath once dead?
It is more than enough to hear of your vigor
in one hand, and of bliss in the other.

In Praise of Abu al-Hassan Shmuel
Ibn Muriel

Are you still longing for your childhood
though your hair's gone white?
And will time swell your mouth with laughter
after you've shed so many tears?
Day after day you write earth a bill of divorce
even while lavishing on her more gifts —
she spits in your face and still you cling to her
after she puts you to shame and removes
your shoe, so why hunger for youth when you've dispatched
the raven, and the dove shrouds your head?
Who has renewed your spirit, and where
does the wind blow that once swept over you?
Who has given the bruised soul
jingling feet and a drumming hand?
So people dare ask me who never set eyes
on the eye that peers from the west,
bright as the orb of a scorchless sun bestowing light.
I won't compare him to the full moon
in its waning, for he waxes and restores
my youth. Appeased, why rage?
An echo bearing myrrh and nectar from the comb
resounds in the halls of wisdom
calling to Shmuel son of Shmuel to rise
and tower over the guests as a crown,
or has Samuel revived and been given true life?
For not as a woman divining, or sorceress,
the vision of the poem gushes out of his mouth
and from his hand gathering its berries —
a poetry that serves his lovers as a balm
and shrivels the hearts of his rivals.

Furtively draw the sword of your reason
and know even the seraphim are scorched by your flame;
not only is merit your nursemaid
but wisdom has become your bondwoman –
be a turban for the public servant,
and for the man of learning a frontlet.

In Seville

He who is raised in a cocoon
cannot imagine his end devoured by maggots.
Fate, passing round its platter of delights
estranges, but I'm no stranger to its ways.
"Honey!" people exclaim smacking their lips.
One sip and I stagger: "Wormwood!"
They insist money grows on trees
yet avoid the tree of knowledge at all cost.
Are you deaf? Fortunate the man
who speaks to attentive ears.
How can you think wisdom burns like coal?
Cupped in your hands – it will turn into a gold band.
But he who craves only sleep never learns,
and God has rendered helpless even
the young lions. How can crouching mules
bear their load when they buckle
under a mere packsaddle? Beasts
that squat on their haunches by the wall
and won't budge have no idea before whom they kneel.
Why believe those who swear in God's name –
they don't know the meaning of the word.
Back off! is how they address God,
refusing to unravel his laws, or fathom
the secret cunning of his paths.
Who can endure for long the company of fools
unless he turns himself into a madman?
– I too, desperate, looking askance
at the sight of so many preening their feathers,
might have despaired were it not for Meir,
who restored my spirits. I planted a seed and found
a harvest of kindness – a crop sown with love.
His hands resemble the tree of life
and the tree of knowledge graces his lips.

His face is the face of a sun that never sets.
He eludes age and exudes learning –
such faultless perfection has never been seen.
Gazing at such precious wine, people ask:
"Where did you find it? In what soil does it grow?"
Had they known his ancestors they would
have said: "Such virtues are handed down
from father to son." His father's honor crowns
his head like Aaron's priestly diadem.

Now I've Become a Burden

Now I've become a burden even to myself.
    How can others bear my distress?
My dear ones have left, seeing
    my eyes dim and the life sapped out of me.
My peers have fled my dark descent
    though they once walked in the light of my rising.
Such were my loves. Who then
    made me reek in the eyes of my companions,
so that even my closest friends
    have betrayed me? Leaving, they've drained
my life-blood, if I go on living
    it is in spite of myself.
I sit alone among simple folk
    who poke fun at my constant whining,
I weep and mourn the stars,
    crying out, alas my brother.
Moshe is set as a seal on my heart
    and Yosef as a frontlet on my forehead.
When I sit down your image sits by me,
    even as your face stares back at me wherever I go.
Your letters are my bosom companions,
    my heart's musings and counsel.
Don't deprive me of them lest you deprive me of life.
    Hold them back and I'm drained
of my strength. So I call out to the passing wind –
    "Bear greetings to my soul's desire
and seize his answer and breathe it into the slain
    by partings, that he may live again."

A Young Girl's Lament from the Grave

Lovely doe, undefiled,
    utterly consumed
still voice in my ears
      underearth
    she who was cast below

My father cast me off
    my brothers forgot me
all drove me
      a deserted soul
    to a desolate land

I said to the pit: you are my father
    called vermin mother and sister

Suddenly summoned
    to make the underworld
my home, borne away
      as death's first-born
    alas I am undone

Clothed in trembling
    in place of choicest garments
beneath linen and brocade

My coat in tatters
    my ear-rings ripped off
my sash and belongings
      snatched from me
    oh weep over my youth

I live boxed in
  among the dead
and know not why

My friends hear
  of my afflictions
renewed each moment
    me eyes tear
  a fire sears my ribs

I hope – without help
  there is no balm in Gilead
nor any physician

All comes to nothing
  for those who dwell on earth
a moment like a blossom wilts
    from house of lyre and lute
  seek the house of mourning

Joys turn
  to cries and sighs
advise and discretion
    to shame and disgrace

Say to whoever asks
  born of the God-fearing
glorious as Ariel's daughters
    keening with the heavenly spheres
  the daughters of Israel set out

Dirge and plaint resounding
  a cloud abiding
the moon confounded
    the sun ashamed

A coal burns me
  a river flows over me
a lion devours me
    father and mother forsake me
    but my lord will gather me

My limbs quake
  my keepers shake
the corpse consumed
    the soul deserted

He calls from his dwelling
  peace to his people
his face will shine
    as she before him
    finds peace in his eyes,

And to her mourners
  overcome with grief
he will bring comfort.

Colloquy

1 *Thrust*

Have you forgotten, love, how you lay in my arms?
    Why have you sold me for good
to my oppressors, when it was I who pursued you
    through barren tracts of land?
Seir, Mount Paran, Sinai, and Sin will bear me out.
    I was yours, and you delighted in me.
How then can you bestow my glory upon others?
    Thrust into Seir, discarded in Qedar,
tested in the Grecian furnace,
    crushed under Medea's yoke. Can there be any savior
but you, any captive of hope but I?
    Give me your strength, I will give you my love.

2 *And Parry*

Ah sleeper, your heart awake, ardently pounding –
    pull yourself together, walk in the light
of my countenance. Rise, ride on, a star strides
    out for you; whoever was down in the pit will ascend
Sinai's summit. Those who say, "Zion is ruined!"
    shouldn't gloat, for my heart and eyes are there;
I reveal, then conceal myself; I rage, and concede.
    Who has more compassion than I for my children?

Distant Dove

A distant dove flutters
    above the treeline, un-
able to break loose,
    lurches, swerves, wings
flapping, whirls
    in a flurry round her lover.
She had thought one
    thousand years
the limit of her time,
    but is confounded
she even harbored such fancies.
    Now her long
absent lover has harrowed
and driven her soul
    to the grave: "Never,"
she swears, "will I mention
    his name again," but no
sooner said and her
    heart kindles like tinder.
Why be her adversary?
    Look how she opens wide
her bill to admit
    the spring shower
of your salvation; believing
    with all her might, never
losing heart – whether
    honored or bowed
down to dust. Surely our
    God shall come,
and not be still –
    round him
tongues of fire rage.

Solomon's Pavilions

Solomon's pavilions, now threadbare and drab among
the dark
goathair tents of Qedar, how you have changed!

"The people who once lodged in our midst left us
defenseless,
a ruin, the holy vessels exiled,
profaned – will you demand splendor of a lily among
thistles?"

Repulsed by their neighbors, sought out by their Lord –
He will summon
them by name, and not one will be missing.

He will restore in the end their glory, as in the beginning,
kindling sevenfold their light in the gloom.

Admonitions

1

Asleep, face nestled in your childhood pillow,
how long will you slumber there?
Mind this: youth is brushed off like fluff.
Imagine such nascent days lasting forever.
Rise, see how your white hairs rebuke you like heralds.
Rid yourself of Time, as birds
shake off last night's dew from their feathers.
             Soar, dart, weave like a swallow,
unconfined, free of your masquerades;
free of the daily surge of events that crest
like the sea. Pursue your King.
– Come, enter the fellowship
of souls flocking to the Lord's bounty.

2

My one and only, seek God on his threshold
and offer your songs as incense

but should you chase after the vanities of your time
and swear such sorcery true

as you moon away your life
and fall into a sweet slumber after a night of pleasure –

know you grasp at nothing
but a bough whose leaves wither tomorrow

stand before your God, your King
under whose wings you've come to take shelter

his name is magnified and hallowed in the mouth of all
who breathe the living breath of God

3

Caught in the iron grip
of my own making,
my vices refuse
to loosen their hold.
Why, my soul, are you cast
down, restless within me?

Youth's follies tie
my heart in knots,
today's pleasures
blur the faces of the dead
as my lute-strings
speak to the winds.

What has my soul
left on this earth?
Only my shame
as great as my sins,
and my praise
as my deeds.

Desire flashes at every
corner, and hope
is dashed. Sated today
tomorrow you'll grieve,
for wretched
are my ways.

But if your path
is straight to your Mover,
a king's bounty
will be your reward –
the one I petition
is no miser.

I Run Towards the Fountain of True Life

I run towards the fountain of true life
    and loathe the false and empty.
My one concern is to see my Sovereign,
    he whom I fear; if only to see
him in my dream, I'd sleep an eternity
    and never wake. If I could only behold
his face within my heart, my eyes
    would no longer seek to gaze abroad.

You Who Knew Me

You who knew me before you formed me,
protect me while your breath is in me.

Can I stand firm if you thrust me aside,
or advance if you block my way?

What can I say when my thoughts are in your hands?
What can I do unless you help me?

I turn to you in times of grace –
answer me, and your grace will shield me.

Wake me to search out your sanctuary –
rouse me to bless your name.

My Soul Craves

My soul craves for the house of God
    and aches, even in dream she ascends
to behold him, ascends but finds no cure
    since dreams can't heal the soul
stricken ill on waking,
    ill the day she didn't implore the face
without whose richness and splendor

she'd wither, wither only to be renewed

straining to rise, for the soul wasn't exiled
    to a void the day she revealed
herself – exiled, she sprung open the fountain gates
    as her gaze fixed on deep waters
fixed to the stake, and bound
    herself by a bond
and vowed a vow, lest she abandon wisdom.

The Penitent

Ever since you were love's encampment
    my love has camped wherever you dwelled.
I delighted for your sake in my rivals' rebuke –
    let them be, as they torment the one
you've tormented. My foes have learned your wrath,
    I love them for hounding the wounded
you've stricken. From the day you scorned me
    I've been filled with self-scorn, for I cannot honor
what you despise until your rage subsides,
    and again you send and restore
the people you redeemed once before.

A Lovely Doe

A lovely doe, why does she laugh
straying far from home,
her lover vexed?
                    She's amused
by the sight of the daughters
of Edom and Arabia,
keen for her lover.
                    Surely those wild
fillies, for all their airs,
can't compare
to the one who once nuzzled
against her gazelle.

                    But who has lately
heard the voice of prophecy,
what has become of ark and lamp,
and of the clinging
divinity?
    Step back, my clamorous
    foes, trying to smother love
    will only fan the flame.

Preciously Abiding

Preciously abiding within the body
    as a flame flickers
      in the gloom
    don't you long to leave
the confines of this frame and come

back to your celestial home?
    Parting, you'll taste
      the fruit of knowledge –
    Edenic, honeyed, sweet
condiments to whet your appetite.

Behold your maker's stately procession
    coming into view and
      forget your past
    afflictions. Praise his name
with every breath: sing to your Lord.

Elohi, How Lovely is Your Dwelling

Elohi, how lovely is your dwelling,
  your nearness manifest, not in dark speeches.
My dream brought me into El's sanctuary,
  and I beheld its handiwork,
its burnt-offerings, grain-gifts and drink-offerings,
  and round about plaited columns of smoke,
and I delighted in hearing the Levites singing,
  each in his turn, in council.
Then I awoke, and still with you gave thanks,
  for it is pleasing to thank you.

Heal Me, My God, and I Will be Healed

Heal me, my God, and I will be healed.
If your anger is kindled, I'll wither!
My potions and drugs are yours –
helpful or harmful, strong or weak.

It is you who chooses, not I,
to you the base and fair are known.
I do not count on my own skills,
but discern your healing powers.

How My Eyes Shine

Day and night extol my Lord, the light
of his face sheds light on my face

he drew up lampwicks and touched darkness
the day he tore windows in the sky

he deigned to invest his majesty in me
his spirit spoke within me through my faithful

he led me on the path where light scattered
as he rose from Seir and came from Sinai

tasting the honey of his faith, I exclaimed
"Come see for yourselves how my eyes shine."

May My Sweet Songs

May my sweet songs and the best part
    of my praise be pleasing in your sight
    love, who wandered far off from me
        because of my wrong doings.
But I grasped the hem of his regard –
    awesome and wondrous. Suffice
    the glory of his name, sole portion
        of all my labor. Increase
my pain, and I will deepen my affection,
    for wonderful is your love for me.

I Lay My Desire

I lay my desire before you, Lord,
    yet dare not raise my voice
and would ask of your favor
    but for a moment – and perish,
if only my request were granted.
    Consigning what's left of my spirit
in your hands, I'll fall into
    the sweetest of slumbers.
Far from you, I die living, but true
    to you, I live though dying,
yet know not how to begin,
    nor how to serve you, nor what
is my faith. Teach me your ways,
    release me from the fetters
of my folly, render me humble
    while yet I stand firm;
don't mock my lowliness
    before I turn burdensome,
even to myself – limb weighing heavy
    upon limb, bowing me down
in submission – for the moth feeds
    on my bones, weary of bearing me up,
as I take to the road my fathers took
    and camp were they encamped,
and wander, a stranger on the earth's
    back, its womb my security.
Once I did as I pleased, but now
    consider the good of my home,
for worldly pleasures you set in my heart
    keep me from seeking my end.
How serve my Maker, hostage
    to my passions, enslaved

to my appetites? Why seek after honor
    when tomorrow the worm
will be my sister? Can my heart rejoice
    on a day of good will, but shun
tomorrow's ills? Day and night
    conspire to consume
my flesh – my better self scattered
    to the wind, my other half returned
to the dust. How speak when lust
    stalks me from youth to old age
like a foe. What have I in life
    other than your favor?
If you aren't my portion, what is?
    I'm stripped of all deeds,
your justice my only covering –
    but why prolong my words,
why question any further? Lord,
    I lay my desire before you.

Revelation

Heavenly spheres beheld your splendor and reeled,
  billows of the deep were stilled
    by your sight, and parted.
  How can souls withstand
    your secret council, where fire sears

and melts boulders. But hearts, take courage
  in you, if you encourage them,
    they will join those who see your glory
  and serve. Therefore souls extol you,
    as praise is fitting and proper.

You Who are Acquainted with Faith

You who are acquainted with faith,
drive out the false, and abide on earth

as he who dwells in the grave.
Serve God in your glory while alive,

and leave time's trappings to others.
Better to rouse the dawn to serve him

then drowse till dawn wakes you.
Weigh tomorrow even today,

don't shudder at leaving the earth to strangers.
Is it not better serving the Lord

than tending to mortals? Let every breath
praise his name recalled with joyful song.

Asleep in the Wings of Wandering

Asleep in the wings of wandering,
   slumbering at the ends
of captivity, all glory spent, I abide
    in a troubled, sullen heart.
       Yet heart restored
        to the gazelle, my spirits revive
       cast off rags of bondage,
        and dress up in pride; my love within,
       I've no use for solid
        ground, or circuit.

When he stands between the torn
   halves of my heart, site
of the throne of honor, need I kin
    or friend – minister or king?
       Should he fear the viper
        when he holds the balm in hand?
       Or the bullock's bellow
        when he commands the strong?
       My creator is mine concealed, I stand
        in his glory's shadow.

Who enters my heart's secret
   council, and, plumbing its depth,
stops the flow of my musings
    on the glory of my King?
       I've treasured up my love
        for my beloved, though he has thrust me
       into the pit, I yield my thoughts
        to him, whether I toil
       or reign, he weighs all actions,
        redeems, or withholds.

I'm free, though I labor
    and laugh mid anguish;
I don't covet a kingdom's splendor,
    nor lack in grace or honor.
        Now I'm consumed with longing
           to dwell in your sanctuary;
      I aspire to stand and serve,
        not to taste your honeycomb,
    nor to pursue covenanter,
      but only attend to your shrine.

My every desire is the foundation
of all foundations, wherein a man
of glory dwells — he is all, and from him comes
all honor and unfailing light.

The Bride Who Longs for You

She steps out to greet you, the bride who longs for you,
and has taken ill ever since she ceased

to shower your precinct with entreaties,
she's astonished whenever she approaches the holy mount

and beholds strangers ascending, and turns back
and stands far off bowing toward your hall

from wherever she may have been exiled
she sends words of supplication to you as an offering

her heart and eyes raised toward your throne –
look down, listen, hear her cry out, brokenhearted, faint

The World was Set Apart

The world was set apart from me
    ever since my soul was precious in my eyes
and she lavished her glory elsewhere
    when she saw the Lord was my portion.

Why should she chose me, her rival –
    or I her, who would lead me to ruin?
I reject her, refuse to take her in, and she,
    removing my shoe, spits in my face.

Startled Awake

Startled awake after dozing off
into troubled sleep – what sort of dream
did you dream? Was it your adversary,
meek and humbled, planted before your disdainful figure?
Tell Hagar's son: "Hold back indignant
your proud hand from your mistress' son!
For I've seen you disgraced and crushed –
if only it were so upon waking,
and 1130 had proved the year of your downfall,
abased and mortified by the plots
you hatched.
          Aren't you the one
people call Wild, whose leaden arm
is all powerful? And haven't they called you
fort en bouche, as you warred
against the Celestial Order. – You
who may rise and stride forth, feet part iron,
part clay, at the end of all days.
If only God would strike you with the stone
that smashed the mold,
making you pay for your past deeds."

Zion, Won't You Ask

Zion, won't you ask after your captives
    who seek your welfare, remnant of your flock?
From west to east, north and south, peace
    from the far and the near, from all sides accept
greetings from desire's captive who offers tears like the dew
    of Hermon, and longs for them to streak your slopes.
I howl like a jackal at your afflictions, but dreaming
    the return of your captivity I'm a lute for your songs.
My heart yearns for Bethel and Penuel, for Mahanaim
    and all the touchstones of your pure ones
where the Shekhinah dwelled near you, and your Maker
    opened your gates before the gates of heaven,
and the Lord's glory was your only light, and neither sun
    nor moon nor stars shone over you.

So I'd pour my life out where the rushing
    spirit of God once drenched your chosen ones;
you are the royal house, the Lord's throne,
    though drudges sit on the thrones of your princes.
If only I could roam through those places where
    God was revealed to your seers and heralds –
who will fashion me wings that I might fly far off,
    brokenhearted, to your mountain clefts?
I'd fling myself down on the ground and treasure
    your stones and favor your dust,
as I stood bewildered by my fathers' tombs
    in Hebron facing the chosen graves,
and walked in your groves and fields and lingered
    in Gilead, astonished at the range beyond –

Mount Avarim and Mount Hor, where two
    luminaries rest, who guide and shine over you.

The air of the land is the life of the soul, myrrh
 is your dust, and honey from the comb your streams.
How I'd delight to tread barefoot and naked
 among the rubble where your shrines once stood:
here is the place where your ark was hidden,
 here the chamber where your cherubim dwelled.
I'd shear off my crown of hair and curse time
 that fouls your saints in an unclean land.
How can I enjoy food or drink when I behold
 curs tearing into your full-grown lions;
how can daylight soothe my eyes while yet
 I see your eagle mangled in the raven's beak.

Gently, cup of sorrow, be still, for even now
 I am filled with your bitterness
and drink your wrath remembering Oholah
 and recalling Oholibah drain your dregs.
Zion, beauty's paragon, bound by love and grace,
 the souls of your peers are joined to you,
they delight in your welfare and, pained
 by your desolation, weep at your shambles.
They long from the pit of captivity and bow,
 each in his place, toward your gates.
The flock of your people, exiled and scattered,
 from mountain to valley, haven't forgotten your folds,
they cling to your fringes and strain
 to climb and clutch the fronds of your palms.

Can Shinar and Patros equal your grandeur?
 Can their spells compare with your Urim and Tummin?
Who is equal to your anointed and prophets,
 and who to your Levites and singers?
The crown of paltry kingdoms perishes,
 but your strength is eternal and your coronal

endures from one generation to another.

God yearns to dwell with you, and blessed the man
set on approaching and abiding in your courts;
    blessed is he who stands and waits, and sees
your light rising as dawn breaks over him, and beholds
    the wealth of your chosen, and rejoices
in your joy when you regain the vigor of your youth.

Earth's Delight and Sovereign City

Earth's delight and sovereign city
    longing from the ends of the west
for your lovely slopes, a tenderness
    stirs within me as I call to mind
your past glory, your dwelling-place
    now in ruin. I'd soar on eagle wings

if only to mix my tears with your dust.
    I go in quest of you, though dispossessed
of your king, and though the scorpion's sting
    has supplanted Gilead's balm.
I will kiss and cherish your stones,
    your earth sweeter to my lips than honey.

Can Lifeless Bodies

Can lifeless bodies
   be chambers
      for hearts lashed
   to eagle wings –
a man at the end of his tether,
   whose only desire
      is to rub his cheeks
   in chosen dust?
He shivers with fear
   and tears well up
      as he casts Spain behind him
   and roams beyond,
first by ship, then foot,
   across parched lands,
      lion dens, leopard mountains.
   Rebuking his friends
he's fixed on wandering,
   abandons home for desert wastes.
      Wolves entice him
   like boys lured
by their sweethearts; he fancies
   ostriches minstrels;
      the roar of lions seems
   like the shepherd's reed;
the fire consuming his guts
   delights him; his tear-ducts
      set torrents free.
   He clambers up hills
and down valleys
   keeping his vow
      he made under oath.
   He camps and decamps

across Zoan, the Egyptian plain,
to Canaan, its chosen range.
His opponents
renew their arguments,
while he listens silently
like no man of words.
How long pit his wit
against them, how long
refute, and why inflict
pain on the besotted?
How could he enjoy
serving royalty,
in his eyes no different
than idolatry?
Like a bird leashed
to a boy's hand,
can a simple, honest man
ever be content
slave to Philistines,
Hagarites and Hittites,
his heart seduced
by other gods
to seek their favor
and forsake God's will,
to betray the Creator
and serve his creatures?
Dawn skies are pitch
black to his eyes,
the sweetest of beverages
bitter to his palate.
Exhausted,
harried and weak,
he yearns for the slopes of Carmel
and Kiryat Yearim,
to seek forgiveness
at the peaceful graves

of ark and tablets
    that lie entombed.

I long to approach
    and grow faint by their tombs,
        eyes brimming
    at their ruins.
All my thoughts
    shudder for Sinai,
        my heart and eyes
    for Mount Avarim.
How can I not
    dissolve into tears
        and hope
    for the dead to revive?
There are the cherubs
    and inscribed tablets –
        among clods of earth
    in a hidden
miraculous place,
    wellspring of prophecy,
        the Lord of Hosts
    shines over them –
I'll cherish its dust,
    And rest beside it,
        and keen
    as over a grave,
the end of all my thoughts
    to lie down
        by my fathers tombs,
    tenanted among the just.

Ride on, ship,
    set keel to land
        where the divine
    presence rooms,

hasten your flight,
  pitched forward
    by God's hand,
  fasten your wings
to dawn's wings,
  they who totter and wander,
    wind clipping the sails,
  hearts torn
into a thousand shreds.
  But I fear
    the sins of youth
  numbered
in the Lord's book,
  and those of old age,
    renewed
  each morning
and cannot answer
  for backsliding,
    and put to straits
  where can I go?
At risk when I forget
  my errors,
    as pith and soul
  yield to sin.
And yet there is trust
  in the lavish in forgiving –
    courage and strength,
  in he who sets the captives free.
Should he judge and pass sentence,
  award or deprive,
    for the good or the bad,
  his judgments stand.

Primed for Flight

Past fifty, and still in pursuit of youth, your days
    primed for flight? Will you flee
from serving God, and long to serve every man,
    seeking the face of many,
but turning from the one within reach
    of all who desire? – Don't delay your journey,
don't give in for a plate of lentils. Hasn't your soul cried
      out, "Enough!"
    as lust yields month after month new fruit.
Incline from its counsel to God-counsel,
    turn away from your five senses, and yield to your
      Creator
for the rest of your days that press on in haste.
    Don't seek with double heart his favor,
don't resort to divination. Be bold as a leopard
    to do his will – light as a gazelle, and strong as a lion.

Midsea, don't be faint-hearted at rolling,
    liquid mountains, the sailors'
hands wrung to tatters, dumbstruck diviners,
    thrilled to scud before the wind,
crushed off course, and buffeted.
    The ocean is your gateway, its razorbacks your refuge.
Sails flap against straining beams,
    winds tease the waves like reapers
pitching sheaves on the threshing floor,
    then stacking them up. When billows crest they're
      lions,
and when toppling a tangle of snakes,
    vipers who won't be charmed.

The hulking vessel is a chip that's pitched in the brine,
    rigging slackens, masts wobble

in their sockets, confusion reigns on deck and below:
    Hands chafe against rope,
men, women, double in pain,
    helmsmen gasp for air, and bodies are drained of life.
Spars are worthless, the elder's counsel
    is brushed aside, cedar masts are stubble,
fir beams reeds, sand-ballast tossed to sea is light as straw,
    iron clasps crumble like chaff.

Each prays aboard ship to his guardian saint,
    while you turn to the Holy of Holies,
and think back to the marvels of the Red Sea and Jordan,
    inscribed – are they not? – on every heart.
You praise the Curber of raging seas,
    as the tides disgorge their mire,
and remind him of the merit of sinful hearts
    while he reminds you of the merit
of the Holy Fathers. If you revive
    the ancient songs and dance,
he will renew his mighty deeds, restore life
    to the dead, flesh to dry bones.

The waves are suddenly silenced, resemble flocks
    scattered in a field, and night –
as the sun steps down galaxies commanded by the moon –
    is a Cushite veiled in gold sequins,
a blue, pearl-spangled brocade.
    The stars are stranded in the sea,
like fugitives driven away;
    their mirror-image streaks the water
and glows like brands of fire.
    Sea and sky – pure, burnished ornaments
of the enveloping night –
    blend into one color, they are two seas
bound together. Between them my heart, a third sea,
    pounds with renewed waves of praise.

My Heart is in the East

My heart is in the east and I'm at the far end of the west.
  How can I taste or savor what I eat?
How keep my vows and pledges – while Zion lies
  shackled to Edom, and I to Arabia bound?
Giving up the riches of Spain would be as easy for me
  as it were precious in my eyes to feast
on dust and rubble of the shrine razed to the ground.

On the Sea

1

Break not, Lord, the breakers of the sea,
nor say to the fathomless gulfs, "Be dry,"
until I repay your kindness, and give
thanks to the western wind and its whitecaps.

Free of Arabia's bond, buffeted
to the shores and thrall of your love,
how can my petitions not come to their end
seeing I trust in you, my surety?

2

Has a flood washed the world to waste?
    Not a scrap of land in sight;
man, beast and fowl, have they gone
under, wrung on the seabed's rack?
What comfort to catch sight
of bluff or shifting sands –
    Even the Libyan desert would please.
Stalking fore-and-aft
    I peer in all directions at nothing
    but water, ark and sky.

                            Leviathan
whitens the surf with age in its churning.
    Drenched in spray, the ship's
snatched by the hands of the thieving sea.
    Waters rage, but I stand firm,
        my spirits raised, Lord,
        drawing near to your sanctuary.

3

Trusting, or flustered, my soul
ever bows to you and assents, rejoices
in you as we weigh anchor,
and gives thanks at every broadside
groan and sigh – as our vessel
plies the sea, sails bellying
out like wings of the stork,
the abyss as though on cue
from my guts, rumbling beneath me,
bringing the sea to a boil;
as swift galleys from Kittim cruise
off the Barbery reefs, and Hittites
lie in wait in their strongholds;
as sea-monsters eye us at meal-time,
and swordfish lance the ship's hull.

Though anguished, like a woman
in labor – panting, unable
to push her firstborn out –
and though lacking food and drink,
the sweetness of your name
is all my nourishment. I've left
my home and property, have no use
for a coffer of riches,
for what is quick to perish;
I've abandoned my daughter,
my kindred spirit and only
child, and it pains me to think
I might forget her son
(whose memory haunts my mind).
Grandson, playmate of my delight,
Can Yehuda ever forget Yehuda?

But these are trifles beside
   your love. Soon I will enter
your gates with thanksgiving
   and there will I dwell
counting my heart as an offering
   on your altar. I'll raise
my headstone in your land –
   proof of my passing.

4

Faint-hearted, knees buckling,
God, I gasp, and break into a sweat.

Oarsmen gape at the deep,

the helmsman lurches, his hands flail,
while I – how could it be
otherwise? – groping for the rail,

dangle between sea and sky.

I reel and stagger. Trifles, if only
I might dance within your walls, Jerusalem.

5

Hard pressed for the Living God, driven
   to search out the thrones of my anointed ones;
denying myself a parting kiss for my child,
   family, companions; not even shedding

a tear over my orchard planted, watered
and pruned to blossom in abundance,
nor letting myself dwell on the memory
of Yehuda and Azariel, two lovely
flowers, the pick of the lot, or Isaac –
sun-ripened fruit, lunar yield –
fancied as my own son. I have all but

forgotten the house of prayer and its study,
my retreat; have ceased
caring for the pleasures of Sabbath,
the charm of my festivals and glory
of Passover. Let others – mere stick figures –
bandy about my high station
and good name. I've swapped my home
for the shadow of a shrub; the bolted security
of my gates, for a low-lying thicket.
Choicest spices sated my palate – now
I reek of thorn bush. I'm through
with scraping and bowing, for I've cut

A path in the heart of the sea. My sights
are set on the Lord's sanctum; there,
on the verge of his holy mountain,
I'll pour out my heart and thoughts,
beneath the doors of heaven, open the flood-
gates of my heart. My spikenard
will flower by the Jordan, my shoots
spread by Shiloah. Adonai is mine. Why should
I fear, since the angel of his mercy
bears my arms? I will extol his name
lifelong, and thank him forever.

6

Tell the heart in the heart of the sea
shaken by the pounding waves:

"Rest assured,
trust in God who made the sea,

his name endures an eternity.

Your fears will subside –
even though the billows swell.

He who curbs the high seas is with you."

7

From heavenly heights
        according to plan,
            he extends
        justice across
distant seas. Man
        treads a road not his
            to own, vain
        his efforts
without His guiding
        hand. Day breaks
            from hollow,
        hastens to cross seas,
thrills like a sprinter
        winning his race.
            Sin lures,
        swerves the ship

off course: though he plead
for the west wind,
east rings
in the shrouds.
With neither will nor power
to hoist the ship's
colors, steer
its course, man repents;
solicitous, humbled
by long service,
bitterly
confesses: Where escape
your spirit, flee
your presence?

Waves whirl, are whipping
tops. Swift clouds
scud over sea.
Sky dims, water
spumes, the deep brims
over and spills
its tide
as the cauldron
hisses unappeased.
Then winds drop
and halve
the watery waste
into mountain crests
and gorges. The ailing
vessel sinks
and rises, eyes
riveted to the sailors,
where are they!
But I hold
my peace, hoping

for the hand of Moses, of Aaron
   and Miriam to draw
      me out; I call
  to my Lord, fearing
my entreaty a burden.

Easterly winds rough up the sea,
   blast the cedar beams;
      gusts scatter
  foam and flotsam. Crew
cower, helmsman
   blanches, yardarm
      strains to spread
  a shroud. Oarsmen
recoil from oar blades,
   despondent, gazing
      at brine
  boiling without fire.
Midshipmen inept,
   deck hands idle,
      the chief-mate's
  brutish, the lookout
blind. The ship scoffs
   and leers, like a sot,
      barters its boarders
  for a song. Now
leviathan from rough
   sea bottom, bids
      like a bridegroom
  his guests to drink –
for the ocean delights
   in its booty;
      and there's no
  shelter, nor
anywhere to flee.

My eyes fail before you,
    Lord, I offer
        supplications
    on your altar;
I shudder
    and yield to you
        Jonah's
    plea; I pluck
a sweet and pleasant
    song of the Red Sea
        rooted
    in memory; I delight
in the deeds
    by the Jordan.
        The heart
    luxuriates as in Eden
to him who sweetens
    the bitter, calms
        disputing
    waters, days of wrath.
Raise your eyes
    to him, cutting a lane
        through high
    seas. His heart
warms the earth,
    his breath chills
        the air.

He has turned his wrath
    from the small
        service vessel,
    bailing it out
of the deep, has hurried
    from on high to calm
        the chasms –
    cries of terror

have ceased. He's churned
   stormy waters
      to butter.
   Gales are swept
away. Passengers
   hear the rustling
      of the angel of mercy –
   a nation tired
of bondage, a storm-
   battered ship,
      hears once more
   a thankful psalm:
Come out from dark clouds,
   faithful daughter,
      the Lord's glory
   shines over you.

8

Greetings ladies, kith and kin,
brothers and sisters, from hope's
captive. Purchased by the high seas,
he's placed himself in the hands
of rival winds: the west wind
steers the ship forward, the levant
whips it back. Between him and death –
a step, a plank. He's trapped
alive in a wooden casket, without earth,
not even a bare four cubits.
He squats to keep his balance,
lies, but cannot stretch his legs,
is sickly, suspicious of strangers,
of pirates and spookish winds.
Helmsman and crew – mere striplings –
are the Pashas and deputies here.

The wise and learned, unless they swim,
have neither honor nor grace.
The thought for a moment clouds my face over
but heart and core thrill, for soon,
at the site of ark and altar,
I'll pour out my soul and render to you,
Lord, who bestows favors on the unworthy,
the pick of my songs and praise.

9

Your breeze, western shore, winged,
fragrant with spikenard and apple,
is released from the spice merchants' sea chest
and not the wind's arsenal. *Be Free,*
you declare, spurring the swallow to flight,
you who are resinous myrrh.
All eyes aboard scan the horizon
for a sign of you who set us
careening over the sea on a plank.
Nightfall or daybreak, don't slacken your hold
on our vessel. Furrow the sea,
slip round the holy mountains, and subside,
rebuking the east wind that fans
the sea to a bubbling cauldron.
What can the captive do,
one moment subdued by the Rock,
the next set free? But my petition's
key is in heavenly hands –
he forges mountains and fathers the wind.

Egypt

Look at the cities, gaze at the unwalled villages
which Israel once held

and honor Egypt – tread lightly,
don't step boldly

down streets where the Matronita passed
seeking the blood-pact on doorposts,

a column of fire and pillars of clouds –
and all eyes kept watch and beheld . . .

from there keepers of the God-pledge were quarried
and founders of Adonai's nation's hewn.

To His Friend and Host Ibn al-Ammani

1

Mountains, desert wastes and seas, send
regards to my grieving friends –
don't let them wring their hands in worry,
for I have been well treated.
I am a nursling in No-amon, in a palace
quarried from the finest of gold,
in Aharon's home, home of the Ark,
a joyful estate of fountains and pools
in a fertile plain, home of a learned friend,
master and judge, just and sincere,
of Jerusalem stock, whose sacred legacy
he received from his forefathers
holy men come from the Temple mount;
born on the spice mountains
he has borne the glory of law and command
as Aaron bore the glory of divination.

2

Stop the surging of the sea until the pupil
draw near and kiss his master's cheek
and hand – Aharon, whose rod
hasn't shattered, nor lost its vigor.
He instructs without telling his mouth: Enough,
dispenses without telling his hands: Too much!
Today I thank the wings of the east
but tomorrow I'm bound to curse the west wind.
How can anyone leave behind him the balm
of Gilead, when stung by a scorpion?
Will he swap the myrtle's shade
For heat, frost and scorching winds?
Rather than the coolness of the master's courtyard
dwell in the shade of the great king's city.

Fate Has Flung Me

Fate has flung me into the wastes of Memphis.
    Go and tell fate: turn me round and hurl me again
until I behold the wilderness of Judah
    and reach the fair heights of the far north
and wrapped in the majesty of Elohi's name
    I'll don the splendor of his holiness, and whirl.

In Alexandria

Has time taken off its clothes of trembling
and decked itself out in riches,
and has the earth put on fine-spun linen
and set its beds in gold brocade?
All the fields of the Nile are checkered,
as though the bloom of Goshen
were woven straps of a breastplate,
and lush oases dark-hued yarn,
and Raamses and Pithom laminated goldleaf.
   Girls on the riverbank, a bevy of fawns,
linger, their wrists heavy with bangles—
anklets clipping their gait.
              The heart enticed
forgets its age, remembers boys or girls
in the garden of Eden, in Egypt, along the Pishon,
running on the green to the river's edge;
the wheat is emerald tinged with red,
and robed in needlework;
it sways to the whim of the sea breeze,
as though bowing in thanks to the Lord . . .

Notes

WHEN HEINRICH BRODY began preparing his edition of
Yehuda Halevi's poetry in 1894, he had at his disposal a
selection of the poet's work edited by the noted Italian
Hebrew scholar, S.D. Luzzatto, and first published in a small
edition (as a wedding gift) in 1840, and, in an expanded
edition, in 1864. The poems in this edition were culled from
a rare manuscript uncovered by the book merchant Eliezer
bar Shlomo in Tunis and purchased by Luzzatto in 1839.
This splendid *diwan* – now in the Bodleian Library in
Oxford – had been compiled by Yehoshua ben Eliahu Halevi,
who lived in the first half of the thirteenth century, possibly
in Yemen. Yehoshua ben Eliahu Halevi, however, was only
the last in a line of four redactors, and in his preface he
writes that the first and most important of Halevi's editors
was Hiyya al-Maghribi, a contemporary of Halevi, who was
most probably the author of the Arabic superscriptions to
many of the poems in the *diwan*. Ezra Fleischer has identi-
fied Halevi's first editor as Hiyya ben Yitzhak, who served as
the *dayyan*, or judge, of Fustat in 1129. In the 1980s a second
diwan, consisting of some seven hundred poems and part of
the Firkovitch collection in St. Petersburg, was made acces-
sible to western scholars. This "New *Diwan*" has proved to
correspond in large part to the *diwan* of Halevi's poems in
the Bodleian Library.

In translating Yehuda Halevi's poetry I have relied on the
following books: the standard four-volume edition of the
poet's work by Heinrich Brody, *Diwan des Abu-l-Hassan
Jehuda ha-Levi* (Berlin: Mekitze Nirdamim, 1894–1930);
Dov Yarden's annotated edition of the liturgical poetry, *The
Liturgical Poetry of Rabbi Yehuda Halevi* (Jerusalem: Volumes
I–IV, 1978–1985); Haim Schirmann's selection appearing in
his anthology *HaShirah HaIvrit B'Sepharad UV'Provence*
(Jerusalem and Tel Aviv: Mossad Bialik and Dvir Co., 1954,
1959); *Jehuda Halevi: Selected Liturgical and Secular Poems,*

edited and annotated by Simon Bernstein (New York: Ogen Publishing House, 1944); *Selected Poems of Jehudah Halevi*, Ed. Heinrich Brody, translated by Nina Salaman (Philadelphia: JPS, 1924); *The Penguin Book of Hebrew Verse*, edited and translated by T. Carmi (New York: Penguin, 1981); *Le Diwan*, translated by Yaacov Arroche and Joseph G. Valensi (Montpellier: Editions de l'éclat, 1988).

Biblical citations in the following notes are not exhaustive. Rather I have tried to offer an aperture on Yehuda Halevi's use of "inlay", or *shibbuts*, the name given by scholars of medieval Hebrew poetry to the delicate weave of scriptural quotations running through a poem. The medieval Arab poets, whose poetry was laced with quotations from the Koran, called the use of koranic citations *iqtibas*, meaning "the lighting of one flame from another". The passage cited, sometimes the shortest of phrases – an epithet, an archaism, an unusual grammatical form – and at other times an entire verse, would more often than not receive in its new setting different and even contradictory shades of meaning. It follows that *shibbuts*, rather than a mere ornamental flourish, not infrequently functioned as a disruptive, probing device. Even the slightest syntactic or lexical adjustments in the quoted inlay were picked up and relished by Halevi's contemporaries, who were, it must be remembered, far more familiar with the Old Testament and its exegesis than we are today: identification and response to recurring instances of *shibbuts* were in all probability second nature, and, as such, immediate and effortless.

Unless otherwise stated, Biblical citations are from the Jewish Publication Society 1917 (JPS) translation *The Holy Scriptures*. On occasion I have relied on the King James Version (KJV), and *Tanakh*, the JPS revised edition of 1985. Verse-references in the JPS edition often differ slightly from the KJV. Marginal references are to the line number of the translation.

A Sleepless Night (*p. 35*)

[Brody I, pp. 159–160]

Adapted from the Arabic.

2   Genesis 33.14: "Let my Lord, I pray thee, pass over before his servant: and I will lead on softly, according as the cattle that goeth before me and the children be able to endure, until I come unto my Lord unto Seir." This verse forms part of the narrative of the reunion and parting between Jacob and Esau.

7–8   Psalms 18.9: "Smoke arose up from His nostrils, and fire out of His mouth did devour . . ."

Cheated (*p. 36*)

1   [Brody I, p. 135]

The superscription in the *diwan* reads: "Translated from an Arabic poem."

2   [Brody II, p. 16]

1   Psalms 72.3: "Let the mountains bear peace to the people, and the hills, through righteousness."

3   Jeremiah 4.30: ". . . that thou enlargest thine eyes with paint?"

4   The staining of fingertips with henna on festive occasions is a common practice to this day in the Middle East.

5–6   Song of Songs 3.5: "that ye awaken not, nor stir up love . . ."

A Reminder (*p. 37*)

[Brody II, p. 21]

4   Song of Songs 2.17: "until the day breathe and the shadows flee away."

To Shlomo Ibn al-Muallim (*p. 38*)

[Uncollected; partial text in Carmi p. 346]

The first half of a panegyric, including an erotic prelude, written in reply to Shlomo Ibn al-Muallim's *qasida* welcoming the young Halevi to Granada. The poem is composed, as was the custom, in the identical meter and rhymes of al-Muallim's panegyric to Halevi. Halevi, however, was not in Granada to receive al-Muallim's poem, and consequently Moshe Ibn Ezra answered the poet with a poem of his own, also set in the identical meter and rhymes, before forwarding al-Muallim's poem to Halevi. In the end Halevi did compose his own panegyric to al-Muallim and the latter poet was graced with two poems of praise.

Shlomo Ibn al-Muallim was born in Seville during the second half of the eleventh century. He moved to Morocco, where he practiced medicine, in the early part of the twelfth century. He was a close friend of Halevi's and his wide learning, knowledge of classical Arabic literature and success as a doctor earned him the honorary title of "Vizier". Maimonides, who knew al-Muallim's son, claimed that al-Muallim was court physician to the Almoravid ruler, Ali Ibn Yusef (1106–1143).

The full text of the *qasida* may be found in S.M. Stern, "Arabic Poems by Spanish-Hebrew Poets", in M. Lazar (ed.), *Romanica et Occidentalia*, Etudes dediees a la memoire de Hiram Peri, Jerusalem 1963, pp. 254–63. Text and commentary in Yehuda Ratzaby, "He Who Seized the Corners of Love", [Hebrew] *Eton* 77, No. 169, February 1994, pp. 16–19.

6   Leviticus 19.19: "Thou shalt not sow thy field with two kinds of seeds."

13   It was customary in Andalusia to perfume one's letters by mixing liquid myrrh into the ink.

15   The biblical Bezalel, the first master craftsman of the Israelites, was responsible for the ornamentation of the Tabernacle. See Exodus 31.2–5.

20   Exodus 7.11: "Then Pharaoh also called for the wise men and the sorcerers; and they also, the magicians of Egypt, did in like manner with their secret arts."

23   Song of Songs 6.3: "I am my beloved's, and my beloved is mine."

25   Psalms 55.8: "Lo, then would I wander far off . . ."

28   Isaiah 19.1: "Behold, the Lord rideth upon a swift cloud, and cometh unto Egypt." Job 36.32: "He covereth His hands with the lightning, and giveth it a charge that it strike the mark."

Wake Up from Your Slumber (*p.* 39)

[Brody II, p. 20]

The superscription in the *diwan* reads: "And he said, as is the custom in love poems, upon seeing his friend asleep." Schirmann adds in his commentary that in medieval Spain a dream was considered "solved", or "divined", if upon waking the dreamer acted out what he had seen in the dream.

Graceful Doe, Pity This Heart (*p.* 40)

[Brody II, pp. 6–7]

A *muwashshah*. These rhymed, strophic poems were composed to be sung and accompanied by music in the eleventh and twelfth-century courts of Andalusia. The end-rhyme in the first three lines of each stanza changed from stanza to stanza, while the last two lines used a fixed rhyme throughout the poem. The final refrain was called a *kharja* and was written – in contrast to the classical diction and meters of the main body of the poem – in the Romance or Mozarabic dialect – a sort of local, streetwise patois. The *kharja* was intended to reproduce the exact speech patterns of a native Andalusian girl of the lower classes. The same *kharja* was frequently used for different poems, and it was believed that the poem was built around the *kharja* and not vice versa ("Holding the tail fast and putting the head on it", in the words of the medieval poet and theorist Ibn Sana al-Mulk). The Hebrew courtier-poets of the day followed suit, adopting into Hebrew the Arabic *muwashshah's* elegant cadences and its courtly themes of unrequited love. They too did not shy away from the elaborate game in which the rhetorical flourishes of the aristocratic class are pitted against the spontaneous outburst in the *kharja* of a young woman. Halevi was a master of this bilingual form and like his contemporaries seems to have taken particular pleasure in embedding key words and phrases from the Bible in an otherwise perfectly profane poem. For an up-to-date study of the *muwashshah* see Tova Rosen, "The Muwashshah" in *The Literature of al-Andalus*, edited by M.R. Menocal, R.P. Scheindlin, and M. Sells (Cambridge: Cambridge University Press, 2000).

2 Genesis 42.4: "But Benjamin, Joseph's brother, Jacob sent not with his brethren; for he said, Lest peradventure mischief befall him." Literally, "Your leaving – or wandering – is my disaster."

4 Proverbs 23.32: "At the last it [wine] biteth like a serpent, and stingeth like an basilisk."

10 Genesis 2.25: "And they were both naked, the man and his wife, and were not ashamed."

16 Psalms 78.65: "Then the Lord awaked as one out of sleep, like a mighty man recovering from wine." New English Bible: "Heated with wine."

22–3 Ezekiel 23.3: "And they committed whoredoms in Egypt; they committed whoredoms in their youth: there were their breasts pressed, and there they bruised the teats of their virginity." Literally, "Remove your hands – for they are inexperienced." Scholars continue to debate the exact meaning of these lines, and of the ensuing *kharja*. Is the subject of the clause the man's hands or the woman's breasts? The old school would have the woman's breasts as untried, while more recent interpretations – based on varient readings of the *kharja* and the recognition of the Andalusian woman's active voice in the *muwashshaha* – have insisted that it is the man's hands that fumble.

24–5 The *kharja*. Haim Schirmann, doyen of Medieval Hebrew scholarship in the mid-twentieth century, translated these lines, written in Romance-Arabic, as follows:

Non me tangas, ya habibi   Don't touch me friend
Yo no kero dan iuso   I don't like those who hurt me

| *Al-gilalatu ruhsatu* | My breasts are soft and sensitive |
| *Bast, a toto me refiuso* | Enough! I shall refuse all! |

The contemporary Israeli critic, Adi Semach, however, has challenged Schirmann's reading of the last line. In its stead he has proposed that the line read, "Bas a tata he permiso", or "Only the nanny does this to me."

A Small Consolation (*p.* 41)

[Brody II, p. 19]

1   Ezekiel 7.20: "And as for the beauty of his ornament, he set it in majesty." Halevi's contemporaries would certainly not miss the irony of the verses that follow the passage from Ezekiel: "But they made the images of their abomination and of their detestable things therein: therefore have I set it far from them." The eponymous *zvi*, or gazelle, is homonymous in biblical Hebrew with the word for "beauty" or "glory", the latter meaning rendered in Ezekiel 26.20: ". . . and I will set glory in the land of the living."

7   Literally, "Whose fragrance is as the frankincense of your nose and mouth." Schirmann glosses the word *adech* as meaning "your mouth", taking his cue from Psalms 103.5: "Who satisfieth thy mouth with good things; so that thy youth is renewed like the eagle's." (KJV). The meaning of the Hebrew, however, is uncertain. The JPS translation renders *adech* as "thine old age", while the revised 1985 *Tanakh* opts for "the prime of life", as does the *New English Bible. Adech* is derived from *ada*, as in Ezekiel 7.20, and stands there for "ornament". *The Hirsch Psalms*, often etymologically acute, renders the verses from Psalm 103 as: "Who satisfies thine ornament with good, until thy youth renews itself like the eagle."

8–9   Numbers 11.7: "and the manna *was* as coriander seed, and the color thereof as the color of bdellium."

Elegy for a Child (*p.* 42)

[Brody II, pp. 149–150]

1   Proverbs 17.21: "He that begetteth a fool doeth it to his sorrow . . ."

2   Job 6.10: "Yea, I would harden myself in sorrow, let him not spare . . ."

3   Job 3.3: "Let the day perish wherein I was born . . ."

4   *Haled*, which I have translated as "rust of this world", denotes "earthly existence", or "the fleeting world", and, in Rabbinic literature, "rust". Cf. Psalms 39.6, where *heldi* is rendered "mine age". See *The Hirsch Psalms* (New York: Feldheim, 1978, p. 291).

5   Genesis 21.16: ". . . 'Let me not look upon the death of the child'".

6   Numbers 6.9: "And if any man die very suddenly beside him, and he defile his consecrated head . . ." I have taken my cue from Everett Fox (*The Five Books of Moses*, London: The Harvill Press, 1995) who renders the line literally as "Suddenly, all-of-a-sudden . . ."

7   Isaiah 1.2: ". . . Children I have reared, and brought up . . ."

8   Job 16.15: "I have sewed sackcloth upon my skin, and have laid my horn in the dust."

9   Ezekiel 28.7: ". . . And they shall defile thy brightness."

11   Proverbs 27.1: "Boast not thyself of to-morrow; for thou knowest not what a day may bring forth."

12   Job 19.21: "Have pity upon me, have pity upon me, O ye my friends; for the hand of God hath touched me."

14   Psalms 38.11: ". . . As for the light of mine eyes, it also is gone from me." Jeremiah 31.20: "Is Ephraim a darling son unto Me? Is he a child that is dandled?"

17   Isaiah 27.3: "I the Lord do guard it, I water it every moment."

18   Jeremiah 4.19: "My bowels, my bowels! I writhe in pain! The chambers of my heart!"

19   1 Samuel 25.37: "And it came to pass in the morning, when the wine was gone out of Nabal, that his wife told him these things, and his heart died within him, and he became as a stone."

In Praise of Shlomo Ibn Ghiyyat (*p.* 43)
[Brody I, pp. 137–141]

Shlomo Ibn Ghiyyat is one of the few poets in Halevi's verse correspondence whose identity has remained shrouded in mystery. Nothing is known of the man, although it is assumed from Halevi's poem, and from the letter in rhymed prose, which Halevi attached to the poem, that Ibn Ghiyyat was considerably older than the poet and was held in high respect. Schirmann has described the poem as "one of the most impressive that the poet wrote in the classical Arab-Andalusian style."

The mono-rhymed *qasida* follows closely, particularly in its opening section (the prelude, or *nasib*), the motifs of the pre-Islamic *qasida*: lamenting the departure of a friend, or beloved, the poet evokes the ruins of the lovers' abode. (Though significantly, following the later development of the *qasida* in Baghdad and in Spain, the ruined encampment is perceived symbolically, as expressive of an inner emotional state.) He then goes on to describe in great detail his own night of sleepless longings, the dramatic appearance of a storm, and finally the long-awaited appearance of dawn. It is only now, at the qasida's midpoint (line 45), that Halevi introduces, along with the first stirrings of a new day, his subject-matter proper: the praise and love of Shlomo

Ibn Ghiyyat, whose own letter and poem Halevi has recently received by carrier-pigeon (the "distant dove stammered – though to me it spoke clearly"). In the final section (lines 71–88) Halevi reiterates his admiration for his friend, laying great stress on his own humble, even inferior position, and announces the dispatching of his verse epistle.

1   Zechariah 4.10: ". . . even these seven, which are the eyes of the lord, that run to and fro through the whole earth."

2   *nedodim* (singular, *nedod*), a key term in medieval Arabic and Hebrew poetry, signifying "separation", "wandering", as in line 5, and "sleeplessness". As for the latter, see the classic treatise on love by Ibn Hazm the Cordovan (994–1069), *The Ring of the Dove*, trans. A.J. Arberry (London: Luzac Oriental, 1994), p. 38: "Sleeplessness too is a common affliction of lovers; the poets have described this condition frequently, relating how they watch the stars, and giving an account of the night's interminable length."

4   Proverbs 1.9: "For they shall be a chaplet of grace unto thy head, and chains about thy neck."

5   Standard motif in classical Arabic poetry, beginning with the sixth-century Imru al-Qais: "Halt, friends both! Let us weep, recalling a love and a lodging by the rim of the twisted sands between Ed-Dakhool and Haumal" (trans. A.J. Arberry). The topos is treated extensively in section IV ("Of Lovers' Pangs and of Houses of Ruin") in Moshe Ibn Ezra's long poem, *Tarshish*.

8   Isaiah 22.5: "Kir shouting, and Shoa at the mount . . ." An obscure passage also rendered, "battering down the wall and a cry (of distress ascends to the mountain)." Jeremiah 4.19: see notes to "Elegy for a Child", line 18.

9   Genesis 42.7–8: "And Joseph saw his brethren, and he knew them but made himself strange unto them."

11   Judges 18.6: "And the priest said unto them, Go in peace: before the Lord is your way wherein ye go."

16   Exodus 15:10: "They sank as lead in the mighty waters."

17   Genesis 3.24: "He drove out the man; and He placed at the east of the garden of Eden the Cherubim, and the flaming sword which turned every way, to keep the way to the tree of life."

21–2   Isaiah 50.11: "Behold, all ye that kindle a fire, that gird yourselves with fire-brands . . ."

24–5   Joshua 7.24: "and the silver, and the mantle, and the wedge of gold . . ."

33   2 Kings 23.11: "And he burned the chariots of the sun with fire."

39   Psalms 73.9: "They have set their mouth against the heavens, and their tongue walketh through the earth." Exodus 9.23: "and the Lord sent thunder and hail, and fire ran along upon the ground . . ."

41–2 Jeremiah 13.23: "Can the Ethiopian change his skin, or the leopard his spots?"

48 Isaiah 28.11: ". . . for with stammering lips and with a strange tongue shall it be spoken to this people." The image of the distant dove, bearing a message of hope under its wings, is frequently used in Halevi's devotional poetry as a symbol for the Congregation of Israel (see "Distant Dove").

50 Cf. Halevi's "Admonitions", 1.

52 Shlomo is the Hebrew for Solomon, who is traditionally regarded as the author of the Song of Songs.

57–8 Song of Songs 4.6: "I will get me to the mountain of myrrh."

59–60 Song of Songs 1.5: "I am black, but comely, O ye daughters of Jerusalem, as the tents of Kedar, as the curtains of Solomon." This motif is treated fully in Halevi's devotional poem "Solomon's Pavilions".

61–2 Allusion to the *Talmud Jerushalmi* where it is written that the *Torah*, which God entrusted to Moses, was engraved in white flames on black fire.

63–4 Proverbs 6.27: "Can a man take fire in his bosom, and his clothes not be burned?" Judges 16.9: "And he broke the bowstrings as a string of tow is broken when it touches fire . . ."

72 Ezekiel 47.12: ". . . it shall bring forth new fruit every month, because the waters thereof issue out of the sanctuary."

75–6 Numbers 11.26: ". . . and they were of them that were written, but went not out unto the tabernacle: and they prophesied in the camp." Halevi puns here on, *ketovim*, the written, which stands for the written teachings in the Old Testament, in contrast to the oral tradition, *masoret*, those teachings handed down after the canonization of the bible.

77 Psalms 113.8: "That He may set him with princes, even with the princes of His people." Job 30.15: "They chase my honor as the wind."

78 Literally, "They are the liver – and he the caul", as in Exodus 29.22: ". . . and the lobe [elsewhere translated as caul] of the liver." The liver was believed to be the seat of the emotions.

80 Psalms 57.9: "Awake, my glory; awake, psaltery and harp; I will awake the dawn." See "You Who are Acquainted with Faith".

83 Exodus 4.10: "And Moses said unto the Lord: 'Oh Lord, I am not a man of words, neither heretofore, nor since Thou has spoken unto Thy servant; for I am slow of speech and of a slow tongue."

84 Exodus 28.13–14: "And thou shalt make settings of gold; and two chains of pure gold." Everett Fox translates "settings" as "braids".

86 Exodus 22.15: "And if a man entice a virgin that is not betrothed, and lie with her, he shall surely pay a dowry for her to be his wife."

After Mutanabbi (p. 46)

[Brody II, p. 16]

The superscription in the *diwan* reads: "Translation adapted from an Arab poem by Mutanabbi." Abu l-Tayyib Ibn Husayn, otherwise known as al-Mutanabbi ("The Pretender to Prophecy") was born in 915 in Kufa and studied in Damascus. He was the court poet of Sayfu l'Dawla at Aleppo between 948 and 957. After a disagreement with his patron he fled to Egypt where he briefly attached himself to the court of the Ikhshidite Kafur and then set off for Baghdad. He was slain by brigands in 965 while traveling through Babylonia. Al-Mutanabbi is generally regarded as one of the great poets of the Arab world.

Three Bridal Songs (p. 47)

There are over fifty extant epithalamiums written by Halevi.

1 [Brody II, p. 318]

–2–3 Song of Songs 5:13: "His lips like lilies, dripping sweet smelling myrrh."

6   Song of Songs 1.6: "Look not upon me, because I am black, because the sun has looked upon me."

2 [Brody II, p. 18]

1   Song of Songs 4.5: "Thy two breasts are like two young roes that are twins, which feed among the lilies." Zechariah 1.8: "I saw by night, and beheld a man riding upon a red horse, and he stood among the myrtle trees."

3   Psalms 59.14: "And let them know that God ruleth in Jacob, unto the ends of the earth."

5   Exodus 25.20: "And the cherubim shall stretch forth their wings on high."

3 [Brody II, p. 37]

The superscription in the *diwan* reads: "And he said in blessing the couple."

5–6 Exodus 30.35: "And thou shalt make of it incense, a perfume after the art of the perfumer, seasoned with salt, pure and holy."

The Fawn (p. 49)

[Brody I, pp. 160–1]

8   Job 14.10: ". . . Yea, man perisheth, and where is he?"

To Yitzhak the Orphan (Ibn Elitom) (*p. 50*)

[Brody I, pp. 82–5]

Itom Hebrew for orphan.

7   Ezekiel 27.7: "Fine linen with richly woven work from Egypt was thy sail . . ."

18   Psalms 78.21: "Therefore the Lord heard this, and was wroth: so a fire was kindled against Jacob, and anger also came up against Israel."

28   Nahum 2.8: "And her handmaids moan as with the voice of doves, tabering upon their breasts."

37–8   A pun on the name Yitzhak (Isaac) which means in Hebrew "to laugh". Cf. Genesis 21.16: "And Sarah said, God hath made me to laugh, so that all that hear will laugh with me."

49–50   Isaiah 32.4: "The heart also of the rash shall understand knowledge, and the tongue of the stammerers shall be made to speak plainly."

59   Psalms 84.4: "Yea, the sparrow hath found an house, and the swallow a nest for herself, where she may lay her young, even thine altars, O Lord of hosts, my King, and my God."

60   Song of Songs 8.5: "Who is this that cometh up from the wilderness, leaning upon her beloved?" *Mitrappequet* (leaning), which I have freely translated as "snuggles", is a *hapax legomenon*, appearing only once in the Bible. See also Halevi's devotional poem "A Lovely Doe", line 11.

Ophra Washes Her Clothes (*p. 52*)

[Brody II, p. 12]

The superscription in the *diwan* reads: "An improvisation composed upon passing by a river where washerwomen were laundering." In keeping with the improvisatory feel of the poem I have allowed myself to stray from the letter of the text. *Ofra* is the Hebrew for a female fawn.

Why Sweetheart Keep Your Envoys (*p. 53*)

[Brody II, pp. 7–10]

The profusion of biblical inlays, particularly verses in which Jerusalem is perceived as the absent beloved (Cf. Psalms 137.5; Jeremiah 2.2), as well as its concluding lines alluding to the Rock of Fortitude, suggest that Halevi may have also been hinting at a religious allegorical reading of this poem. Dan Pagis has observed that the poem reverses the conventional figure of the rejected suitor by portraying "true lovers, in body and soul: though now compelled to part, they know that their love is timeless." See Dan Pagis, *Hebrew Poetry of the Middle Ages and the Renaissance*. (Berkeley: University of California Press, 1991, p. 14).

1   Isaiah 57.9: "And thou wentest to the King with ointment, and didst increase thy perfumes, and didst send thy messengers far off, and didst debase thyself even unto hell."

6   Psalms 17.15: "As for me, I will behold Thy face in righteousness: I shall be satisfied, when I awake, with beholding Thy likeness."

8   Genesis 13.3: "And he [Abram] went on his journeys from the south even to Beth-el . . ."

13–14 Isaiah 51.15: "For I am the Lord thy God, who stirreth up the seas, that the waves thereof roar."

18   Exodus 28.33–34: "A golden bell and a pomegranate, a golden bell and a pomegranate, upon the hem of the robe round them."

27   Proverbs 4.16: "For they sleep not, except they have done evil; and their sleep is taken away, unless they cause some to fall."

29   1 Kings 18.38: "Then the fire of the Lord fell, and consumed the burnt sacrifice, and the wood, and the stones, and the dust, and licked the water that was in the trench."

35   Exodus 39.3: "And they did beat the gold into thin plates . . ."

40   Literally, "cloud of your hair".

51   Song of Songs 5:1: "I have eaten my honeycomb with my honey."

53–4 Song of Songs 8.6: "Set me as a seal upon thine heart, as a seal upon thine arm."

55–6 Psalms 137.5: "If I forget thee, O Jerusalem, let my right hand forget her cunning." Jeremiah 2.2: "Go and cry in the ears of Jerusalem, saying: Thus saith the Lord: I remember for thee, the affection of thy youth, the love of thine espousals, how thou wentest after Me in the wilderness, in a land that was not sown."

63   Genesis 37.7: "For, behold, we were binding sheaves in the field, and lo, my sheaf arose, and also stood upright, and, behold, your sheaves stood round about, and made obeisance to my sheaf."

69–70 Exodus 32.34: "Behold, my angel shall go before thee; nevertheless in the day when I visit, I will visit their sin upon them." Isaiah 26.19: "The dead men of thy people shall live, my dead body shall arise."

76   Ezekiel 16.3: "And say, Thus saith the Lord God unto Jerusalem: thine origin and thy nativity is of the land of the Canaanite." Psalms 107.30: "Then were they glad because they were quiet, and He led them unto their desired haven."

Bear Arms Against the Victim (*p.* 56)

[Brody II, p. 34]

Schirmann has remarked on the thematic similarities between this petitionary love lyric and the devotional poem "The Penitent", where initially the lover wholeheartedly identifies with the beloved's rejection and in almost identical language encourages her cruelty.

1   Proverbs 7.26: "For she hath cast down many wounded; yea, a mighty host are all her slain. This chapter of Proverbs deals specifically with the figure of the temptress.

8   Song of Songs 4.11: "Honey and milk are under thy tongue."

On Parting from his Friend Moshe Ibn Ezra (*p. 57*)
[Brody I, pp. 154–7]

Born in Granada in 1055, Moshe Ibn Ezra was the doyen of Hebrew letters in Andalusia during Halevi's youth [see introduction]. Ibn Ezra fortunes would change drastically after the occupation of the city by the Berber Almoravids. Legend has it that he embroiled himself in a liaison with the daughter of his elder brother, and that in fleeing the city and seeking refuge in Christian Spain he was escaping as much the wrath of his brother as the sword of the Almoravids. What is certain (Ibn Ezra makes a number of allusions to the matter in his verse written in exile) is that two of his brothers refused to help him during his years of expatriation, and that even his children behaved, as Heinrich Brody has put it, "in an unfilial manner toward their father." For the next forty years Moshe Ibn Ezra led the checkered life of a vagabond, drifting from city to city – Toledo, Saragossa, Barcelona, Seville – and yearning bitterly for the company of old friends, for the children he had left behind, and for his beloved Granada. He died some time after 1135.

2   Judges 5.21: "The river Kishon swept them away, that ancient river, the river Kishon . . ."

7   Psalms 8.4: "When I behold Thy heavens, the work of Thy fingers."

9   Psalms 77.11: "And I say: 'This is my weakness, that the right hand of the Most High could change.'"

13–15   A gloss on the biblical accounts of Babel (Genesis 11.1–9) and the birth of Jacob and Esau (Genesis 25.23).

17   Proverbs 3.8: "It shall be health to thy navel and marrow to the bone."

25   Literally, "Like my eyes on the day the cloud rested upon them." Exodus 40.35: "Then Moses was not able to enter into the tent of the congregation, because the cloud abode thereon, and the glory of the Lord filled the tabernacle."

34–5   Song of Songs 5:13: "His cheeks are as a bed of spices. As banks of sweet herbs." A literal translation of line 35 would read: "Sucking the breasts of the daughter of the vineyards" – a stock phrase in medieval Arabic and Hebrew poetry for describing the drinking of wine. Isaiah 66.11: "That ye may suck, and be satisfied with the breast of her consolations."

36   Songs of Songs 2.17: "Turn, my beloved, and be thou like a gazelle or a young hart upon the mountains of spices [of Bether]." The last word has been variously interpreted as "division, separation", as a proper name, an aromatic plant, or, allegorically, as alluding to the covenant (*brit* in Hebrew), as in Genesis 15:10, where the Hebrew stem *b-t-r*, "to sever" stands for the division or cutting of the sacrificial pieces.

38   Literally, "tears defiled with blood". Isaiah 9.4: "For every boot stamped with fierceness, and every cloak rolled in blood, shall even be for burning, for fuel of fire."

42   Psalms 55.22: "Smoother than cream were the speeches of his mouth, but his heart was war."

52–3   Genesis 37.7: "For, behold, we were binding sheaves in the field, and, lo, my sheaf arose, and also stood upright; and, behold, your sheaves came round about, and bowed to my sheaf."

54   Proverbs 11.22: "As a jewel of gold in a swine's snout, so is a fair woman which is without discretion."

Coda (*p.* 59)
[Brody I, pp. 92–3]

A separate poem, which I have taken the liberty of placing as an adjunct to the longer poem.

4   Numbers 17.28: "Every one that cometh near, that cometh near unto the tabernacle of the Lord shall die; shall we wholly perish?"

5   Song of Songs 2.17: Cf. line 36.

8–9   Song of Songs 8.6: Cf. lines 53–4, "Why Sweetheart Keep Your Envoys". Zephaniah 3.9: "For then will I turn to the peoples a pure language that they may call upon the name of the Lord, to serve him with one consent."

11   2 Samuel 1.21: "Ye mountains of Gilboa, let there be no dew nor rain upon you, neither fields of choice fruits; for there the shield of the mighty was viley cast away, the shield of Saul, not anointed with oil." Halevi's grief over Moshe Ibn Ezra's departure is compared here to David's lament over the death of Saul and his son, Jonathan.

Wine Songs (*p.* 60)

The wine poem was not so much an excuse for debauchery, as some have suggested, as a highly developed literary genre whose courtly origins are to be found in the poetry of Abu Nuwas (757–814). The setting – a flowering garden in springtime, or the warm interior of one's patron's home in winter – and the occasion – light entertainment, song and dance, and wine passed round in a circle – offered the opportunity for a poet to hone his wit in poems that reflected on the passage of time and embodied, in Christopher Middleton's words, a "Sensory multiplicity of the aesthetic phenomenon" (see *Andalusian Poems*, translated by Christopher Middleton and Leticia Garza-Falcon, Boston: David Godine, 1993). Thus the beauty of the young cupbearer – male or female – was extolled in loving detail, as were the hues and pungency of the wine, the crystal transparency of the goblet, the fragrance and festive attire of flowers in the garden, the changing colors of the skies at dusk or at dawn, and the pleasing voices of the guests that blended with the sounds of the lute and bird song.

1 [Brody II, pp. 308–9]

1   Judges 5:12: "Awake, awake Deborah; awake, awake, utter song."
9–10 In the last two lines Halevi plays on the Hebrew word *cad*, which means "jug", and consists of two Hebrew letters that have the numerical value of twenty-four, apparently the poet's age at the time of the poem's composition.

2 [Brody II, p. 243]

4   Lamentations 4.7: "They were more ruddy in body than rubies."
7   Exodus 2.3: "And when she could no longer hide him, she took for him an ark of bulrushes, and daubed it with slime and with pitch, and put the child therein . . ."
9–10 Genesis 9.12: "And God said, this is the token of the covenant which I made between me and you and every living creature that is with you for perpetual generations."
12   A playful pun – substituting "raven" with "striking" – on the Talmudic proverb: "Not for nothing did the starling follow the raven, it is of its kind." [Birds of a feather flock together].

The Night My Doe (*p.* 61)
[Brody II, p. 20]

Even in this miniature, perhaps improvised at a garden party, a critical ear would catch in Halevi's use of the word *nesheph* for "dawn" in the last line a playful allusion to Job 7.4: ". . . and I am full of tossings to and fro unto the dawning of the day."

To Shlomo Ibn Feruziel upon Returning from Aragon (*p.* 62)
[Brody I, pp. 14–15]

The superscription in the *Diwan* reads: "In praise of Rabbi Shlomo Ibn Feruziel, Cidellus sister's son, upon returning from Aragon."

Shlomo Ibn Feruziel was the nephew of the noted vizier and physician to Alfonso VI, Joseph Ibn Feruziel, surnamed Cidellus. The Christian nobles of Castile and the Jewish community held Shlomo and his uncle in the highest esteem. He was murdered by Christian mercenaries in 1108, as he returned from Aragon where he had been sent on a diplomatic mission. Halevi, who had set out to compose a poem celebrating his return, was now constrained into abruptly lamenting the sudden death of his friend. Upon completion of this poem Halevi wrote a brief elegy to his friend: "Ah, this is not a day of good tidings, friend, / as you were told of the murder of Shlomo / turn, heart, your song into an elegy / to his rending on the day he hoped for peace" [Brody II, p. 92]. Even such an "improvised composition", as the quatrain is called in the Arabic superscription, is replete with Biblical allusions (2 Kings 7.9, Psalms 30.12, Isaiah 30.13, and Jeremiah 8.15). Halevi delicately plays on the name Shlomo which can mean as well, in a slightly altered form, but retaining the same phonetic identity, "his peace", or "his welfare".

The first section is spoken, or rather sung, by a young woman plaintively strumming a lute, or *oud.*

1   Nahum 3.4: "... the mistress of witchcrafts, that selleth nations through her harlotries ..."

29–30   I have followed here Brody's reading of these lines, which might be rendered literally as "When she let fall a crystal into the water of her tears my own eyes dissolved at the dazzle of the pearls of her treasure". Schirmann offers the alternative reading of *enai l'bechai peneni dam atodia,* "My eyes dissolved [at the sight of] her tears, blood-pearls from her treasure", and comments: "When the pain is intensified the heart's blood is mixed with tears and they turn red. The poet is so moved by the sight of the beautiful woman crying that he too sheds red tears, drawn from the treasure of her tears."

Riddles (*p.* 64)

[Brody II, pp. 205; 196; 195]

No. 1   A quill. Ink was commonly called at the time, according to Schirmann, *the blood of idols.*

No. 2   A needle.

No. 3   A hand mirror.

Impromptu (*p.* 65)

[Brody II, p. 316]

4   1 Samuel 30.8: "And David inquired at the Lord, saying, Shall I pursue after this troop? Shall I overtake them? And He answered him, Pursue: for thou shalt surely overtake them, and without fail recover all."

The Sons of Fortune (*p. 66*)

[Brody II, pp. 318–9]

1   Literally, "sons of days", a common medieval coinage in Arabic and Hebrew designating fate, though the more frequently used term is "Daughters of days".

2   Daniel 12.9: "And he said: 'Go thy way, Daniel; for the words are shut up and sealed till the time of the end.'"

4   Proverbs 12.4: "A virtuous woman is a crown to her husband; but she that doeth shamefully is rottenness in his bones."

5–6   Genesis 41.22–23: "And I saw in my dream, and, behold, seven ears came upon one stalk full and good. And, behold, seven ears, withered, thin, and blasted with the east wind, sprung up after them."

16   Job 28.18: "No mention shall be made of coral or of crystal; yea, the price of wisdom is above rubies."

19–20   Psalms 16.11: "In Thy presence is fullness of joy, in Thy right hand bliss for evermore."

In Praise of Abu al-Hassan Shmuel Ibn Muriel (*p. 67*)

[Brody I, pp. 129–131]

Ibn Muriel is described by Simon Bernstein in his edition of Halevi's poetry as follows: "This Shmuel, it appears, who was in his youth a poet and *payytan* and had abandoned poetry as a result of personal setbacks and tribulations, returned to composing poems in his old age. Yehuda Halevi greets him as a great poet and defends him against those who criticize him for daring to return to "The love of his youth" after all his failures and disappointments."

5   Deuteronomy 24.1: "When a man taketh a wife, and marrieth her then it cometh to pass, if she find no favour in his eyes, because he hath found some unseemly thing in her, that he write her a bill of divorcement . . ." This line has posed textual difficulty. I have followed Brody's reading, which suggests that the poet initiates daily a divorce (albeit reluctantly) from earthly pleasures. Shaul ben Abdallah Yosef, however, in his important commentary on Yehuda Halevi's poetry, *Givat Shaul* [Hebrew] (Vienna: Unger, 1923), proposes an alternative reading: "Day after day earth writes you a bill of divorcement."

6   Literally, "adds to her bride-money".

7–9   Deuteronomy 25.9–10: See notes to "The World Was Set Apart" for the application of Jewish laws of re-marriage. Compare as well lines from "I Roused My Sleeping Mind" by Moshe Ibn Ezra: "And so I scorn this world and shun her lure, / so that she not pile sins on me –/ abandon her, lest she abandons me, / untie

my shoe, fling spittle in my face . . ." (trans. Raymond
Scheindlin).

9–10   Genesis 8.7–9: "And he sent forth a raven, and it went forth to
and fro, until the waters were dried up from off the earth. And
he sent forth a dove from him, to see if the waters were abated
from off the face of the ground." The raven and dove, were stock
images in Arabic and Hebrew poetry not only of night and day
("until the white dawn rises like a dove", writes Moshe Ibn Ezra,
"from beneath the wings of a raven that flees away") but also of
dark-haired youth and white-haired age. Halevi applies the same
theme in a lighthearted quatrain: "The day a dove nestled in a
raven's nest / I said, poor creature ensnared / better a raven's
blackness in the morning / than a dove's brilliance at dusk."
[Brody II, p. 216].

11   Psalms 51.12: "Create me a clean heart, O God; And renew a
steadfast spirit within me."

14   Isaiah 3.16: "Walking and mincing as they go, and making a
tinkling with their feet . . ."

16   Song of Songs 6.10: "Who is she that looketh forth as the dawn
. . ." It was customary to refer to Andalusia as "the west".

24   2 Chronicles 3.15: ". . . and the capital that was on the top of each
of them was five cubits."

25   Samuel the prophet.

26   1 Samuel 28.7: "Then said Saul unto his servants: 'Seek me a
woman that divineth by a ghost, that I may go to her, and
inquire of her."

33   Leviticus 19.20: "And whosoever lieth carnally with a woman,
that is a bondmaid, designated for a man . . ."

36   Exodus 13.16: "And it shall be for a sign upon thy hand, and for
frontlets between thine eyes; for by strength of hand the Lord
brought us forth out of Egypt." "Man of learning", literally
"man of the Torah"; "frontlet": phylactery.

In Seville (*p.* 69)

[Brody I, pp. 127–9]

The superscription in the *diwan* reads: "And he castigated the commu-
nity of Seville and then went on to praise the vizier Abu el-Hassan
Meir Ibn Kamniel."

Abu el-Hassan Ibn Kamniel was a member of a wealthy and highly
respected family in Seville with ties both to the Jewish and Muslim
communities. Later in life he moved to Morocco, where he practiced
medicine in the Almoravid courts of Fez.

Seville had long been considered "the city of poets", but shortly
before Halevi's visit to the city-state, its poet-king al-Mutamid called
in the Almoravids to help repel the advance of the Christian Alfonso

144

VI. The Almoravids were so successful in their military campaign that they decided to stay on in Andalusia, permanently. Consequently al-Mutamid, who had once declared "he preferred to be a camel driver in Morocco rather than a swineherd in Castile", was packed off to Tangiers, his feet fettered, to die in exile. Seville now became an object of scorn, its poets impoverished and abandoned by the court.

1   Lamentations 4.5: "They that did feed delicately are desolate in the streets: they that were brought up in scarlet embrace dunghills."

6   Isaiah 51.17: "Awake, awake, stand up, O Jerusalem, that hast drunk at the hand of the Lord, the cup of His fury; even the cup of staggering, and drained it."

15   Psalms 58.7: "Break their teeth, O Lord, in their mouths: break out the great teeth of the young lions, O Lord."

22   Job 21.14: "Therefore they say unto God, Depart from us, for we desire not the knowledge of Thy ways."

27   Schirmann has suggested that Halevi may be alluding to his own financial straits as a young poet, shortly after leaving Granada.

28   Psalms 75.6: "Lift not up your horns on high; speak not insolence with a haughty neck."

42   Exodus 28.40: "And for Aaron's sons thou shalt make tunics, and thou shalt make for them girdles, and head-tires shalt thou make for them, for splendor and for beauty."

Now I've Become a Burden (*p.* 71)

[Brody I, pp. 26–7]

Addressed to Yitzhak Ibn Ezra, though his younger brothers, Moshe and Yosef, are also mentioned. Yitzhak Ibn Ezra had moved to Cordova after the defeat of Granada.

1   Job 7.20: "Why hast Thou set me as a mark for Thee, so that I am a burden to myself?"

2   Deuteronomy 1.12: "How can I myself alone bear your cumbrance, and your burden, and your strife?"

3   Daniel 9.23: ". . . for thou art greatly beloved; therefore look into the word, and understand the vision." *Chamoodot*, "beloved". The Hebrew uses the abstract form, literally: "loveliness, delights". I have followed Brody's reading of this word as meaning "Precious friends", though an alternate reading would suggest that Halevi is mourning the loss not of friends but of his own passions, or charms. Hebrew allows for the reader to entertain both meanings.

4   Deuteronomy 34.7: "And Moses was a hundred and twenty years old when he died: his eye was not dim, nor his natural

force abated." Cf. line 4 of "To His Friend and Host Aharon Ibn al-Ammani", 2.

6   Isaiah 60.3: "And nations shall walk at thy light, and kings at the brightness of thy rising."

8   Exodus 5.21: ". . . the Lord look upon you, and judge; because ye have made our savour to be abhorred in the eyes of Pharaoh . . ."

14   Job 30.1: "But now they that are younger than I have me in derision . . ."

24–5   Daniel 10.8: "So I was left alone, and saw this great vision, and there remained no strength in me."

26   "soul's desire": *machmad roochi*. Same root as *chamoodot* of line 3: *chamad*: "desire, desirable thing".

27–8   Ezekiel 37.9: "Then said He unto me: 'Prophesy unto the breath, prophesy, son of man, and say to the breath: Thus saith the Lord God: Come from the four winds, O breath, and breathe upon these slain, that they may live.'"

A Young Girl's Lament from the Grave (*p.* 72)

[Brody II, pp. 146–8]

3   1 Kings 19.12: ". . . but the Lord was not in the fire; and after the fire a still small voice."

5   Genesis 39.1: "And Joseph was brought down to Egypt, and Potiphar, an officer of Pharaoh's, the captain of the guard, an Egyptian, brought him of the hand of the Ishmaelites, that had brought him down thither . . ."

6   Psalms 60.3: "O God, Thou hast cast us off, Thou has broken us down."

9   Joel 2.20: ". . . and will drive him into a land barren and desolate."

10   Ezekiel 32.15: "When I shall make the land of Egypt desolate and waste, a land destitute of that whereof it was full . . ." The Hebrew plays on the homonyms *neshama, neshama*, the former meaning "soul" (or "spirit", "breath"), and the latter "desolate".

11–12   Job 17.14.

16   Job 18.13: "Yea, the first-born of death shall devour his members."

18   Ezekiel 26.16: "they shall clothe themselves with trembling . . .". Cf. line 1 of "In Alexandria".

19   Genesis 27.15: "And Rebekah took the choicest garments of Esau her elder son . . ."

20   Ezekiel 16.13: "Thus was thou decked with gold and silver; and thy raiment was of fine linen, and silk, and richly woven work . . ."

33   Jeremiah 17.4: ". . . for ye have kindled a fire in My nostrils, which shall burn for ever."

35–6   Cf. line 7 in "Wine Songs", 1, line 10 in "Earth's Delight and Sovereign City", and lines 10–11 in "To His Friend and Host Aharon Ibn al-Ammani", 2.

37   "Ecclesiastes 1.14: "And, behold, all is vanity and a striving after wind."

38   Isaiah 18.3: "All ye inhabitants of the world, and ye dwellers on the earth."

40–41 "Ecclesiastes 7.2: "It is better to go to the house of mourning, then to go to the house of feasting."

50   Judges 11.40: "And it was a custom in Israel that the daughters of Israel went yearly to lament the daughter of Jephthah the Gileadite four days in a year."

52   Job 3.5: "let a cloud dwell upon it . . ."

53–4   Isaiah 24.23: "Then the moon shall be confounded, and the sun ashamed . . ."

58–9   Psalms 27.10: "For though my father and my mother have forsaken me, the Lord will take me up."

61   "Ecclesiastes 12.3: In the day when the keepers of the house shall tremble."

63   See line 10.

66   Numbers 6.25: "The Lord make His face to shine upon thee . . ." Part of the Priestly Benediction in the Jewish liturgy.

67–8   Song of Songs 8.10: "Then I was in his eyes as one that found peace."

71   Isaiah 57.18: "I will lead him also, and requite with comforts him and his mourners."

Colloquy (p. 75)

"*Thrust*" and "*And Parry*" are separate poems placed side by side as a dialogue between Israel and God. Such antiphonal interchanges between *Knesset Yisrael* (the Congregation of Israel) and God were a common poetic practice in the writing of devotional poems to be sung during services in the synagogue.

Thrust
[Brody III, p. 4]

A *reshut*, or introductory petition, in this case for *nishmat* ('the breath'), the first text of the Saturday liturgy. It was written for *Rosh Hashana*, the Jewish New Year, and served to introduce the prayer beginning "Let all souls [that breathe] praise the Lord." The initial letter of each line forms the acrostic Yehuda.

1   Literally, "between my breasts", as in the Song of Songs: 1.13: "My beloved is unto me a bundle of myrrh which lieth betwixt my breasts."

3–4   Jeremiah 2.2: ". . . I remember thee, the kindness of thy youth, the love of thine espousals, when thou wentest after Me in the wilderness, in a land that was not sown."

5   Seir, Mount Paran, Sinai, Sin, are all biblical locations where God appeared or spoke to the Israelites.

8–10   Seir, Qedar, the Grecian furnace, Media: as in the four kingdoms which appear in Belshazzar's dream in Daniel. In medieval Hebrew poetry Seir stood for the Christian nations since it was the land promised to Esau, whose redness became the purple of Imperial Rome and of the Roman Catholic Church. Qedar was equated with the Muslim nation [see notes to "Solomon's Pavilions"], and Media with Persia.

And Parry
[Brody III, p. 67]

A *reshut*, written for *Shavuot*, the Feast of the Weeks. Halevi assumes the voice of the Lord speaking to his nation.

1   Song of Songs 5.2: "I sleep, but my heart waketh: it is the voice of my beloved that knocketh, saying Open to me, my sister, my love, my dove, my undefiled . . ." Traditional Jewish exegesis interprets these lines allegorically: God awakens Israel out of its moral and mental slumber. The *Targum* reads: "After all these words, the people of the House of Israel sinned, and He delivered them into the hand of Nebuchadnezzar, King of Babylon, and he led them into exile and in the exile they resembled a man who slumbers and cannot be aroused from his sleep. Then the voice of the Holy Spirit enlightened them by means of the prophets and It [or She] aroused them from the slumber of their mind."

2–3   Judges 16.20: ". . . And he awoke out of his sleep, and said, I will go out as at other times before, and shake myself . . ." Psalms 89.16: "Blessed is the people that know the joyful sound: they shall walk, O Lord, in the light of Thy countenance." Numbers 24.17: "Then shall come a star out of Jacob, and a scepter shall rise out of Israel."

6   1 Kings 9.3: "I have hallowed this house, which thou hast built, to put My name there forever; and Mine eyes and My heart shall be there perpetually."

7   Isaiah 54:8: "In a little wrath I hid My face from thee for a moment; but with everlasting kindness will I have compassion on thee, saith the Lord thy Redeemer."

8   Malachi 3.17: "And they shall be Mine, saith the Lord of hosts, in that day which I make my peculiar day, and I will spare them, as a man spareth his own son that serveth him."

Distant Dove (*p.* 76)

[Brody IV, pp. 274–5]

A *selihah*, or penitential song, to be read, in the Ashkenazic synagogue, during the forty nights preceding Yom Kippur (The Day of Atonement). The historian Yosef Yerushalmi discusses the importance of *selihot* in his book *Zakhor: Jewish History and Jewish Memory* (Seattle: University of Washington Press, 1982, p. 45): "The single most important religious and literary response to historical catastrophe in the Middle Ages was not a chronicle of the event but the composition of *selihot*, penitential prayers, and their insertion into the liturgy of the synagogue. Through such prayers the poet gave vent to the deepest emotions of the community, expressed its contrition in face of the divine wrath or its questions concerning divine justice, prayed for an end to suffering or vengeance against the oppressor, and in effect, 'commemorated' the event."

The acrostic Yehuda Levi is formed by the initial letter of each line.

1   Psalms 56.1: "For the leader; upon Jonath-elem-rehokim [a distant dove], a michtam of David, when the Philistines took him in Gath." The dove is here a symbol for *Knesset Yisrael*, the Congregation of Israel.

7–8   One thousand years – since the destruction of the Temple.

12–15 Isaiah 53.12: "Because he bared his soul unto death."

19   Jeremiah 20.9: "Then there is in mine heart as it were a burning fire shut up in my bones . . ."

27–9 Job 14.21: "His sons come to honor, and he knoweth it not; and they are brought low, but he regardeth them not."

29–32 Psalms 50.3: "Our God shall come, and shall not keep silent: a fire shall devour before him, and it shall be very tempestuous round about him." (KJV)

Solomon's Pavilions (*p.* 77)

[Brody IV, p. 82]

A *me'ora*, or "light hymn", praising God for locating the 'luminaries' – the sun and moon. Sung during the Sabbath *Hazon*, the Sabbath after the 9th of Av. It precedes the closing formula of the first benediction before the *Shema*, affirming the unity of God: "Hear, [*Shema*] O Israel, the Lord is our God, the Lord is One" (Deuteronomy 6.4). As a rule the *me'ora* interprets "light" or "luminary" symbolically as the light of the Torah, of Providence, and the redemption of Zion.

1–2   Song of Songs 1.5: "As the tents of Kedar, as the curtains of Solomon." Kedar was a tribe of northern Arabia. The root *qdr* connotes darkness or blackness. Halevi employs the curtains (*yeriot*) as a metonym for the destroyed temple of Jerusalem.

Lamentations 4.1: "How is the gold become dim! How is the most fine gold changed!"

5 Song of Songs 2.2: "As a lily among thorns."

6–7 Isaiah 40.26: "He calleth them all by names; because of the greatness of His might, and because He is strong in power, not one faileth."

8–9 Daniel 11.29: "But it shall not be as the former, or as the latter." Isaiah 30.26: "And the light of the sun shall be sevenfold . . ." Ezekiel 32.8: "And all the lights of heaven will be made dark over thee."

Admonitions (*p.* 78)

The first two poems are petitions for *nishmat* in which the poet urges the soul to lead a purer, more exalted life. The third poem is a *pizmon*, or hymn, its stanzas resembling a *muwashshah*.

1 [Brody III, pp. 226–7]

1 Proverbs 6.9–10: "How long wilt thou sleep, O sluggard? When wilt thou rise out of thy sleep." Cf. Solomon Ibn Gabirol: "You who tarry in the bosom of youth, wake up! Don't sleep for all the days of youth vanish like smoke."

5 Genesis 19.14: "And Lot went out, and spoke unto his sons-in-law who married his daughters and said: 'Up, get you out of this place; for the Lord will destroy the city.'"

7 Isaiah 52.2: "Shake thyself from the dust; Arise and sit down, O Jerusalem; loose thee from the bands of thy neck, O captive daughter of Zion"; Song of Songs 5.2: "For my head is filled with dew my locks with the drops of the night."

8 Psalms 84.4: "Yea, the sparrow hath found a house and the swallow a nest for herself where she may lay her young . . ." The Hebrew for "swallow" (*dror*) can also stand for "freedom" and "myrrh".

12–13 Jeremiah 31.12: "And they shall come and sing in the height of Zion, and shall flow unto the goodness of the Lord."

2 [Brody III, p. 145]

The acrostic Yehuda is formed from the initial letter of the first five lines of the poem.

1 Psalms 22.21: "Deliver my soul from the sword; mine only one from the power of the dog." Psalms 78.34: "When He slew them, then they would inquire after Him, and turn back and seek God earnestly."

2 Psalms 141.2: "Let my prayer be set forth as incense before Thee . . ."

6 Jeremiah 31.26: "And my sleep was sweet unto me."

10   Ruth 2.12: "The Lord recompense thy work, and a full reward be given thee of the Lord God of Israel, under whose wings thou art come to trust."

11   Ezekiel 38.23: "Thus will I magnify and sanctify Myself; and I will be known in the eyes of many nations, and they shall know that I am the Lord."

12   Genesis 7.22: "And in whose nostrils was the breath of life, of all that was in the dry land, died."

3 [Brody III, pp. 174–5]

1   Lamentation 3.7: "He hath hedged me about, that I cannot get out: he hath made my chain heavy."

5–6   Psalms 42.6: "Why are thou cast down, O my soul? And why are thou disquieted within me? Hope thou in God: for I shall yet praise Him for the help of His countenance."

7–8   Psalms 25.7: "Remember not the sins of my youth, nor my transgressions." Proverbs 22.15: "Foolishness is bound in the heart of a child . . ."

12   Literally, "vanities of my vanity". Cf. Ecclesiastes 1.2.

30   I have followed Schirmann's reading of *clai*, "my instrument", to stand for "a generous and large-hearted God" Yarden, however, offers an alternative reading based on Isaiah 32.7: "The instruments also of the churl of evil." Yarden paraphrases the poems concluding line as follows: "man cannot expect to escape the instrument of his evil inclinations."

I Run Towards the Fountain of True Life (*p.* 81)
[Brody III, p. 118]

1   Psalms 36.10: "For with Thee is the fountain of life; in Thy light do we see light."

3   Exodus 33.18–23: "And he said, I beseech thee, shew me thy glory . . . And He said, Thou canst not see My face: for there shall no man see Me, and live . . . And I will take away My hand. And thou shalt see My back parts: but My face shall not be seen."

7   The word *beita*, derived from *beit*, "house", and here signifying "inward", or "inner", is used in Ezekiel 44.19 to describe the inner court of the restored temple; similarly in Exodus 28.26 it is applied to the ephod, worn by the high priest.

You Who Knew Me (*p.* 82)
[Brody III, pp. 116–7]

A *reshut l'borechu*, petition for "The blessing" as indicated in the last line "to bless your name", written for Succoth, the Feast of Tabernacles.

Raymond Scheindlin offers an illuminating comparison (see *The Gazelle: Medieval Hebrew Poems on God, Israel, and the Soul*, Philadelphia: Jewish Publication Society, 1991, pp. 208–17) between this petition and Ibn Gabirol's magnificent "Before My Being". Although both poets begin with the same biblical citation from Jeremiah, Ibn Gabirol's poem is characteristically turbulent and paradoxical in its understanding of the body's – and the soul's – agonistic relation toward the creator, whereas Halevi's more intimate strains convey a sense of profound trust and acceptance of a transcendent being. See Peter Cole's *Selected Poems of Solomon Ibn Gabirol* (Princeton: Princeton University Press, 2001, p. 111.)

1   Jeremiah 1.5: "Before I formed thee in the belly I knew thee . . ."
4   Isaiah 22.19: "And I will thrust thee from thy post . . ."
5   Joshua 7.8: "Oh Lord, what shall I say . . ."
7   Isaiah 49.8: "In an acceptable time have I answered thee . . ." Psalms 69.14: "But as for me, let my prayer be unto Thee, O Lord, in an acceptable time . . ."
8   Psalms 5:13: "For Thou dost bless the righteous; O Lord, Thou dost encompass him with favor as with a shield." Psalms 41.11: "But Thou, O Lord, be gracious unto me, and raise me up, that I may requite them."

My Soul Craves (*p. 83*)

[Brody II, pp. 306–7]

This poem, as well as "Preciously Abiding", emerges from Muslim Neoplatonic thought, especially as such teachings were reintegrated in the writings of Ibn Gabirol and Bahya Ibn Pakuda – the latter Halevi's contemporary – where the human soul, fallen from the divine order, seeks to re-ascend to its celestial palace. Halevi, however, takes comfort not only in the good counsel of Proverbs – and here biblical citations work as a powerful undersong – but also in Isaiah's prophecy of rejuvenation and Ezra's 'little space of grace" found amidst the temple's ruins. The last allusion suggesting that the soul's exile and yearning for the House of God may be understood equally as the yearning of the Congregation of Israel for the restoration of its Temple. In the Hebrew, alternating lines begin with the last word of the preceding line. For a textual-theological analysis of this poem see Franz Rosenzweig (in Barbara Ellen Galli, *Franz Rosenzweig and Yehuda Halevi, Translating, Translations, and Translators*. Montreal, McGill-Queen's University Press, 1995, p. 214).

1–2   Psalms 84.3: "My soul yearneth, yea, even pineth for the courts of the Lord . . ."
9–10   Isaiah 45:18: "For thus saith the Lord that created the heavens; God himself that formed the earth and made it; he hath established it, he created it not in vain, he formed it to be inhabited . . ."

The *Tanakh* offers these lines as, "He did not create it a waste, but formed it for habitation . . ."

11 Isaiah 41.18: "I will open rivers in high places and fountains in the midst of the valleys . . ."

12 Proverbs 20.5: "Counsel in the heart of man is like deep waters; but a man of understanding will draw it out."

13 Ezra 9.8: "And now for a little space grace hath been shewed from our Lord, our God, to leave us a remnant to escape and give us a nail in His holy place. That our God may lighten our eyes, and give us a little reviving in our bondage."

13–15 Numbers 30.3–4: "If a woman also vow a vow unto the Lord, and bind herself by a bond, being in her father's house in her youth; and her father hear her vow . . . and every bond wherewith she hath bound her soul, shall stand." Cf. "My Heart is in the East", line 3.

The Penitent (*p.* 84)
[Brody IV, p. 232]

Luzzatto, with his usual perspicacity, pointed out in his edition of the *diwan* that the extreme contrition of this poem is not typical of Jewish thought, suggesting that the poem was adapted from outside Arabic sources. Israel Levin has indeed demonstrated that the poem is in effect a translation – with the exception of the last line – of a ninth-century Arabic love lyric by Abu al-Shis. See Israel Levin, "I Sought the One Whom My Soul Loveth" [Hebrew], *Hasifrut* 3 (1970–1971), pp. 116–49. Raymond Scheindlin has further demonstrated that the poem in Arabic was anthologized by the Andalusian Sufi, Ibn al-Arif, a contemporary of Halevi.

The emotions expressed here find their parallel in *The Kuzari*, translated from the Arabic by Hartwig Hirschfeld (New York: Schocken Books, 1964, p. 79):

"The Rabbi: Thou hast touched our weak spot, O King of the Khazars. If the majority of us, as thou sayest, would learn humility towards God and His law from our low station, Providence would not have forced us to bear it for such a long period. Only the smallest portion thinks thus. Yet the majority may expect a reward, because they bear their degradation partly from necessity, partly from their own free will. For whomever wishes to do so can become the friend and equal of his oppressor by uttering one word, and without difficulty. Such conduct does not escape the just Judge. If we bear our exile and degradation for God's sake, as is meet, we shall be the pride of the generation which will come with the Messiah, and accelerate the day of the deliverance we hope for."

4–7 Psalms 69.27: "For they persecute him whom Thou has smitten;

and they talk to the grief of those whom Thou has wounded."

10–11 Deuteronomy 9.26: "I prayed therefore unto the Lord, and said, O Lord God, destroy not Thy people and Thine inheritance, which Thou has redeemed through Thy greatness, which Thou has brought forth out of Egypt with a mighty hand.

A Lovely Doe (p. 85)

[Brody IV, p. 230]

An *ahava* ("love"): prologue to the second morning benediction ("Who has chosen His people Israel with abounding love") read before the *Shema*.

1 The doe represents the *Knesset Yisrael*, the Congregation of Israel.

8–9 Genesis 16.12: "And he shall be a wild ass of a man: his hand shall be against every man, and every man's hand against him."

11 Song of Songs 8.5: "Who is this that cometh up from the wilderness, leaning upon her beloved."

16–17 The *Shekhinah*: feminine aspect of God as developed in Jewish mystical texts.

Preciously Abiding (p. 86)

[Brody IV, p. 177]

A *reshut* for *nishmat*. The acrostic Yehuda is formed out of the initial letter of the first five lines of the poem. Speaking of the soul in *The Kuzari* [p. 102] Halevi writes: "As a symbol of the Divine Influence, consider the reasoning soul which dwells in the perishable body. If its physical and nobler faculties are properly distributed and arranged, raising it high above the animal world, then it is a worthy dwelling for the King Reason, who will guide and direct it, and remain with it as long as the harmony is undisturbed."

2–3 Job 38.19: "Where is the way to the dwelling of light . . ." Jeremiah 2.31: "O generation, see ye the word of the Lord, have I been a wilderness unto Israel? Or a land of thick darkness?"

7–8 A pun on the word *predah* which may be read as "parting" and, if halved into two words, *pree datah*, "fruit of her knowledge".

10 Psalms 103.5: "Who satisfieth thy mouth [JPS: "thine old age"] with good things." See notes to "A Small Consolation", line 7.

Elohi, How Lovely is Your Dwelling (p. 87)

[Brody II, p. 160]

The superscription in the *diwan* reads: "And he said in describing a dream he saw." *Elohi*: My God. *El* is used in the Bible and in other ancient Semitic languages as a proper name for God. The destroyed Temple is the poetic topos for the expression of loss and homelessness in Rabbinic literature.

1   Psalms 84.2: "How lovely are Thy tabernacles, O Lord of hosts!"

2   Numbers 12.8: "... with him do I speak mouth to mouth, even manifestly, and not in dark speeches ..."

5   Numbers 29.6: "... beside the continual burnt-offering, the meal-offering thereof, and the drink-offering thereof."

9   Psalms 139.18: "... Were I to come to the end of them, I would still be with Thee."

Heal Me, My God, and I Will be Healed (*p.* 88)
[Brody II, p. 294]

The superscription in the *diwan* reads: "And he said after drinking some medicine." It should be remembered that Halevi was himself a practicing physician. This short poem is based on one of the petitions in the weekday *amidah* ("Standing"); a core prayer recited three times daily.

2   Judges 6.39: "Let not Thine anger be kindled against me."

How My Eyes Shine (*p.* 89)
[Brody III, pp. 74–5]

A *yotser*, "Who creates [*yotser*] light and forms darkness", inserted in the first daily blessing prior to the morning *Shema*, which reflects on daybreak and blesses the daily renewal of creation. The acrostic Yehuda is formed out of the initial letter of each line.

1   Exodus 13.21: "And the Lord went before them by day in a pillar of cloud, to lead them the way; and by night in a pillar of fire, to give them light; that they might go by day and by night ..."

2   Exodus 25.37: "And thou shalt make the lamps thereof, seven; and they shall light the lamps thereof, to give light over against it."

3   Exodus 25.37: see above; I have relied here on Everett Fox's interpretation of *he'elah nerot*, "drew up lampwicks", appearing in his translation of the Pentateuch. Exodus 10.21: "And the Lord said unto Moses: 'Stretch out thy hand toward heaven, that there may be darkness over the land of Egypt, even darkness which may be felt.'"

4   Jeremiah 22.14: "That saith: 'I will build me a wide house and spacious chambers,' and cutteth him out windows ..." The grammatical form of windows, *chalonai*, is unusual in this

passage, and might also be read as "my windows". Cf. the Sabbath and Festival *yotser* prayer that begins "All Will Thank You" and continues: "The God that opens every day doors of the Gates of the East and pierces windows of heaven, who brings out the sun from its place and the moon from its dwelling-place and shines over the entire world."

5   Numbers 27.20: "And thou shalt put of thy honor upon him . . ."
6   2 Samuel 23.2: "The spirit of the Lord spoke by me, and His word was upon my tongue."
7   Job 38.24: "By what way is the light parted, or the east wind scattered upon the earth?"
8   Deuteronomy 33.2: "The Lord came from Sinai, and rose from Seir unto them . . ."
9–10   1 Samuel 14.29: "Then said Jonathan: 'My father hath troubled the land; see, I pray you, how mine eyes are brightened, because I tasted a little of this honey.'"

May My Sweet Songs (*p. 90*)
[Brody IV, p. 222]

An a*hava*, for insertion in the blessing before the *Shema*. The acrostic Yehuda is formed out of the initial letter of each line.

3   Psalms 55.8: "Lo, then would I wander far off, I would lodge in the wilderness."
4   Deuteronomy 28.20: ". . . because of the evil of thy doings, whereby thou hast forsaken Me."
5   1 Samuel 15.27: "And as Samuel turned about to go away, he laid hold upon the skirt of his robe, and it rent."
6   Psalms 139.14: "I will give thanks unto Thee, for I am fearfully and wonderfully made . . ."
7–8   Psalms 79.9: "Help us, O God of our salvation, for the sake of the glory of Thy name . . ." Ecclesiastes 2.10: ". . . and this was my portion from all my labor."
8–9   Ecclesiastes 1.18: "For in much wisdom is much grief: and he that increaseth knowledge increaseth sorrow." Yehuda Razhabi has pointed to the confluence of Jewish and Muslim sources in these lines, referring to Proverbs 9.8 "Reprove a wise man and he will love thee", as quoted in the Talmudic tractate *Arachim*, and to the Muslim poet al-Mutanabbi's verse: "Go on [increase] harming my soul, and I will increase my love for you / for what burns in man is the hateful desirer." Similar lines are also to be found in *The Book of Direction to the Duties of the Heart* (trans. Menahem Mansoor, London: Routledge & Kegan Paul, 1973, p. 428), by the influential Jewish pietist Bahya Ibn Pakuda: ". . . My God, You have made me hungry and naked, and You have put

me in the darkness of night. But I swear by Your power and greatness, that were You to burn me with fire, it would only add to my love for You and my attachment to You." See Yehuda Razhabi, "Borrowed Elements in the Poems of Yehuda Halevi from Arabic Poetry and Philosophy" [Hebrew], *Molad* 5 (1973), pp. 166–75.

10   2 Samuel 1.26: ". . . Wonderful was thy love to me, passing the love of women." The concluding line of David's lament for Jonathan.

I Lay My Desire (*p.* 91)
[Brody III, pp. 266–8]

A *bakasha*, or supplication, inserted in the Yom Kippur liturgy. As is customary with many poems of supplication, the poem opens and ends with the same line.

1   Psalms 38.10: "Lord, all my desire is before Thee . . ."

2   Literally, "Even though I do not bring it to my lips." Ezekiel 36.3: "And ye are taken up in the lips of talkers . . ."

3–4   Psalms 30.6: "For His anger is but for a moment, His favor is for a life-time . . ."

5   Job 6.8: "Oh that I might have my request . . ."

6–8   Psalms 31.6: "Into Thy hand I commit my spirit . . .". Jeremiah 31.26: "Upon this I awakened, and beheld; and my sleep was sweet unto me." Cf. "Admonitions", 2, line 6.

13   Psalms 25.4: "Show me Thy ways, O Lord; teach me Thy paths."

17   Psalms 22.25: "For He hath not despised nor abhorred the lowliness of the poor . . ."

18–20   Job 7.20: ". . . So that I am a burden to myself?" Cf. Abu Nuwas: "I see myself as alive and among the living, though most of myself is dead . . . what isn't dead bears what is dead . . . my limbs having become a grave for my limbs." Cf. Ibn Gabirol: "You are a body in which limbs are consumed by limbs and soon will return to the worm and dust."

21–2   Psalms 31.11: "My strength faileth because of mine iniquity, and my bones are wasted away." Isaiah 51.8: "For the moth shall eat them up like a garment, and the worm shall eat them like wool . . ." Isaiah 1.14: "Your new moons and your appointed seasons My soul hateth: They are a burden unto Me; I am weary to bear them."

25   Genesis 23.4: "I am a stranger and a sojourner with you . . ."

28   Genesis 30.30: "And now when shall I provide for mine own house also?"

29   Ecclesiastes 3.11: "also He hath set the world in their heart . . ." *Kohelet Rabba* and Avraham Ibn Ezra interpret these lines as

"The love of the world", or, in the latter case, as one's "appetite or hunger for the world."

34–5 Job 17.14: "If I have said to corruption: 'Thou art my father,' to the worm: 'Thou art my mother, and my sister.'"

35–6 Judges 19.9: "lodge here, that thy heart may be merry . . ." Ecclesiastes 7.14: "In the day of prosperity by joyful, and in the day of adversity consider . . ."

38 Literally, "surety", or "pledge", as in Genesis 43.9: "I will be surety for him; of my hand shalt thou require him . . ."

42–3 Genesis 18.12: "And Sarah laughed within herself, saying: 'After I am waxed old shall I have pleasure, my lord being old also?'"

45 Psalms 16.5: "O Lord, the portion of mine inheritance and of my cup, Thou maintainest my lot."

46 Micah 1.8: "I will go stripped and naked . . ."

47 Exodus 22.26: "For that is his only covering, it is his garment for his skin . . ."

Revelation (*p. 93*)

[Brody III, p. 3]

A *reshut* for *nishmat*, recited during the first days of Passover.

5 Jeremiah 23.18: "For who hath stood in the council of the Lord . . ."

6 Psalms 31.25: "Be strong, and let your heart take courage, all ye that wait for the Lord."

9–10 Psalms 150.6: "Let every thing that hath breath praise the Lord. Hallelujah."

10 In the Hebrew God is addressed as *Elohim*: traditional evocation of God's name as justice-maker. Psalms 147.1: "Hallelujah; for it is good to sing praises unto our God; for it is pleasant, and praise is comely." Psalms 33.1: ". . . Praise is comely for the upright."

You Who are Acquainted with Faith (*p. 94*)

[Brody III, p. 143]

A *reshut* for *nishmat*, for the eighth day of Succoth, the Feast of Tabernacles. The acrostic Yehuda is formed from the initial letter of the first five lines.

1 Isaiah 53.3: "A man of pains, and acquainted with disease." Proverbs 28.20: "A faithful man shall abound with blessings."

2 Isaiah 26.19: "Awake and sing, ye that dwell in the dust."

4 Psalms 45.4: "Gird thy sword upon thy thigh, O mighty one, Thy glory and thy majesty." Psalms 104.33: "I will sing unto the Lord as long as I live; I will sing praise to my God while I have any being."

6–7 Psalms 57.9: "Awake, my glory; awake, psaltery and harp; I will awake the dawn." *Talmud Yerushalmi, Berachot*: "I would wake the dawn, and dawn would not wake me."

10 1 Samuel 2.18: "But Samuel ministered before the Lord, being a child, girded with a linen ephod."

11–12 Psalms 150.6: Cf. "Revelation", line 9–10. This is the last line in the Book of Psalms. Isaiah 26.8: ". . . To Thy name and Thy memorial is the desire of my soul." Genesis 31.27: "Wherefore didst thou flee secretly, and outwit me; and didst not tell me, that I might have sent thee away with mirth and with songs, with tabret and with harp . . ."

Asleep in the Wings of Wandering (*p. 95*)
[Brody III, pp. 152–3]

A *meora* for insertion at the end of the *yotser*, written for *Simhat Torah*, in the form of a *muwashshah*. The acrostic Yehuda is formed from the initial letter of the first refrain, the first line of each stanza, and the last refrain. See notes to "The Bride Who Longs for You".

1 Psalms 55.8: "Lo, then would I wander far off, I would lodge in the wilderness."

4 1 Kings 20.43: "And the king went to his house sullen and displeased . . ."

9–10 A collation of two passages from Job: 22.14: "And He walketh in the circuit of heaven", and 38.38: "When the dust runneth into a mass, and the clods cleave fast together."

11–12 Genesis 15:10: "He brought Him all these and cut them in two, placing each half opposite the other . . ." Jeremiah 34.18: "And I will give the men that have transgressed My covenant, that have not performed the words of the covenant which they made before Me, when they cut the calf in twain and passed the parts thereof . . ." Jeremiah 17.12: "Thou throne of glory, on high from the beginning, thou place of our sanctuary . . ." The throne of glory is traditionally associated with the Temple which was regarded as God's terrestrial throne. Halevi imagines the heart as both the loci of the biblical covenant-making ceremony and of the divine essence, symbolized by the throne. The latter image is indebted to early *merkavah* or chariot-mysticism, see Elliot R. Wolfson, "Merkavah Traditions in Philosophical Garb: Judah Halevi Reconsidered", *Proceedings of the American Academy for Jewish Research* Vol. LVII, 1990–1991, pp. 179–242.

18 Judges 5:13: "Then made He a remnant to have dominion over the nobles and the people; the Lord made me have dominion over the mighty."

19–20 Psalms 91.1: "O thou that dwellest in the covert of the Most

High, and abidest in the shadow of the Almighty."

21–2   Jeremiah 23.18: "For who hath stood in the council of the Lord . . ."

26–7   Psalms 88.7: "Thou hast laid me in the lowest pit, in darkness, in the deeps."

32   Proverbs 31.25: ". . . and she laugheth at the time to come."

35   Psalms 119.20: "My soul breaketh for the longing . . ."

39   Daniel 11.22: "And the arms of the flood shall be swept away from before him, and shall be broken; yea, also the prince of the covenant." The allusion in the Book of Daniel is to the High Priest of Jerusalem during the reign of the Seleucid Antiochus IV. Halevi is perhaps drawing a parallel between the unstable court and city-state alliances of his day in Andalusia and those of the Hellenized Jews in second century Palestine.

41   2 Samuel 23.5: "For all my salvation, and all my desire, will He not make it to grow?"

44   Zephaniah 3.5: "Every morning doth He bring His right to light, it faileth not."

The Bride Who Longs for You (*p. 97*)

[Brody III, p. 144]

A *reshut* for *Simhat Torah*. The acrostic Yehuda is formed from the initial letter of the first line of each couplet. In this festival, which celebrates the completion of the yearly reading of the Pentateuch, the *Hatan Torah* (Bridegroom of the Torah) is symbolically wedded to the Torah.

1   Proverbs 7.15: "Therefore came I forth to meet thee, to seek thy face, and I have found thee."

4   1 Samuel 1.7: "And as he did year by year, when she went up to the house of the Lord . . ."

6–7   1 Kings 8.48: ". . . if they return unto Thee with all their heart and with all their soul in the land of their enemies, who carried them captive, and pray unto Thee toward their land, which Thou gavest unto their fathers, the city which Thou hast chosen, and the house which I have built for Thy name."

10   Deuteronomy 26.15: "Look forth from Thy holy habitation, from heaven, and bless Thy people Israel . . ." Psalms 84.3: "My soul longeth yea, even fainteth for the courts of the Lord."

The World was Set Apart (*p. 98*)

[Brody II, p. 292]

Jewish marriage law, dealing with a widow's claim on her brother-in-law, and his possible rejection of that claim (Deuteronomy 25.5–10), form the background to this compact, eight line parable of man's rejection of the material world.

1 The word *neda* is usually translated as "unclean", or "impure", as in Leviticus 20.21: "And if a man shall take his brother's wife, it is impurity . . ." and Ezra 9.11: "The land unto which you go to possess it, is an unclean land . . .". However, *neda* may mean as well "cast out", "banished", "set apart".

2 1 Samuel 26.21: "Because my life was precious in thine eyes this day."

3 Isaiah 42.8: "I am the Lord, that is My name; and My glory will I not give to another."

4 Lamentations 3.24: "The Lord is my portion, saith my soul . . ."

6 Ezekiel 7.19: ". . . because it hath been the stumblingblock of their iniquity."

7–8 Literally, "I am brother-in-law and have no desire to take her / and she removes [my shoe] and spits in my face." Halevi is alluding to Deuteronomy 25.5–10: "If brethren dwell together, and one of them die, and have no child, the wife of the dead shall not be married abroad unto one not his kin; her husband's brother shall go in unto her, and take her to him to wife, and perform the duty of a husband's brother unto her . . . And if the man like not to take his brother's wife, then his brother's wife shall go up to the gate unto the elders, and say: 'My husband's brother refuseth to raise up unto his brother a name in Israel; he will not perform the duty of a husband's brother unto me.' Then the elders of his city shall call him, and speak unto him; and if he stand, and say: 'I like not to take her'; then shall his brother's wife draw nigh unto him in the presence of the elders, and loose his shoe from off his foot, and spit in his face; and she shall answer and say: 'So shall it be done unto the man that doth not build up his brother's house.' And his name shall be called in Israel The house of him that had his shoe loosed."

Startled Awake (*p.* 99)

[Brody II, p. 302]

The Arabic superscription in the *diwan* reads: "And he said of what he saw in his dream."

2–3 Genesis 37.10: "What is this dream that thou has dreamed?"

9 1130. Halevi, following the custom of the day, tries his hand at fixing the date of the redemption. How the poet arrived at this date is explained by Raymond Scheindlin in *The Gazelle*, p. 111, from which I quote: "Halevi's method is a sort of number divination, by which the year of redemption is derived from the numerical value of the Hebrew letters *tts* (=890). Halevi must

have chosen to base his calculation on these letters because they represent the year in which the dream occurred, if it was a real biographical event, or, if it was merely a fiction, the year in which he composed the poem. Since the thousands are ordinarily dropped in citing the Hebrew dates, 890 would have meant to Halevi 4890 AM, corresponding to AD 1129–30. The three Hebrew letters in turn spell the Hebrew word *titos*, 'you will overturn'. The root occurs in several biblical prophecies of doom, as in God's original charge to Jeremiah: 'See, I appoint you this day over nations and kingdoms: To uproot and to pull down, to destroy and to overthrow, to build and to plant.'" 1130 was also the year in which the Berber Almohads conquered North Africa and devastated its Jewish communities. For Jews living in Andalusia this was a sign of impending doom (which indeed occurred in 1140, the very same year that Halevi sailed to Egypt, when the Almohads invaded the south of Spain).

13 Genesis 16.12: "And he shall be a wild ass of a man." Cf. "A Lovely Doe", lines 8–9.

15 Daniel 7.8: "And a mouth speaking great things." Part of a vision of the fourth monstrous beast of Daniel 7 and written in Aramaic, which is the language of six chapters of the Book of Daniel. I have consequently chosen to recreate a parallel effect by shifting into French.

17–20 Daniel 2.33–34: "His legs of iron, his feet part of iron and part of clay. Thou sawest till that a stone was cut out without hands, which smote the image upon his feet that were of iron and clay, and brake them to pieces." Nebuchadnezzar's dream. Halevi reverts again to a pastiche of Aramaic and Hebrew.

Zion, Won't You Ask (*p.* 100)
[Brody II, pp. 155–8]

A *kina*, or dirge, sung during the synagogue services on the 9th of Av (*Tish'a b'Ab*) when, according to tradition, both the First and the Second Temple were destroyed. Halevi's poem gained near iconic status outside of the synagogue service in the eighteenth and nineteenth centuries. Translated into numerous languages, it was appropriated by German Romantics, Haskalah reformists and Jewish nationalists who saw in its fervor and unrestrained longing for a homeland an echo of their own strivings for a religious-national identity. After reading Johann Gottfried von Herder's translation, published in 1791, Goethe would write with admiration of the poem's rare "fire of longing".

3–5 Isaiah 57.19: "I create the fruit of the lips: Peace, peace to him that is far off, and to him that is near, saith the Lord; and I will heal him."

11   See note to "A Lovely Doe", lines 16–17.

15–16 Job 30.16: "And now my soul is poured out within me." The Hebrew word *ruah* can mean both "wind" and "spirit" and is translated as such ("rushing-spirit") in Everett Fox's rendering of Genesis 1.2.

21   Psalms 55.7–8: "And I said, oh that I had wings like a dove, for then I would fly away, and be at rest. Lo, then I would wander far off, and remain in the wilderness. Selah."

22   Song of Songs 2.17. Cf. "On Parting from his Friend Moshe Ibn Ezra", line 36.

23–4 Psalms 102.15: "For Thy servants take pleasure in her stones, and favor the dust thereof."

33   Isaiah 20.3: "And the Lord said, like as my servant Isaiah hath walked naked and barefoot three years for a sign and wonder upon Egypt and Ethiopia."

37   Jeremiah 7.29: "Cut off thine hair, and cast it away, and take up a lamentation on the high hills."

41   Ecclesiastes 11.7: "And the light is sweet, and a pleasant thing it is for the eyes to behold the sun."

45–6 See Ezekiel 23 for a description of Ohalah and Oholibah, who "played the harlot."

47   Lamentation 2.15: "Is this the city that men call the perfection of beauty, the joy of the whole earth?"

55   1 Samuel 15.27: "And as Samuel turned about to go away, he laid hold upon the skirt of his mantle, and it rent." Cf. "May My Sweet Songs", line 5.

56   Song of Songs 7.9: "I said: I will climb up into the palm-tree, I will take hold of the branches thereof . . ."

57   Shinar and Patros, biblical names for Babylonia and Egypt.

58   Urim and Tummin. See notes to "To His Friend and Host Aharon Ibn al-Ammani."

61–3 Proverbs 27.24: "For riches are not for ever; and doth the crown endure to every generation."

64   Psalms 132.13: "For the Lord hath chosen Zion; He hath desired it for His habitation."

65   Psalms: 65.5: "Happy is the man whom Thou chooses, and bringest near, that he may dwell in Thy courts." The terms *choose* and *bring near* are used in the priestly ordination, as in Numbers 16.5.

66   Daniel 12.12: "Happy is he that waiteth, and cometh to the thousand three hundred and five and thirty days."

69   Ezekiel 16.55: "When thy sisters, Sodom and her daughters, shall return to their former estate, and Samaria and her daughters, shall return to their former estate, then thou and thy daughter shall return to your former estate."

Earth's Delight and Sovereign City (*p.* 103)

[Brody II, pp. 167–8]

The initial letter of each line forms the acrostic Yehuda.

1   Psalms 48.3: "Fair in situation, the joy of the whole world; even mount Zion, the uttermost parts of the north, the city of the great King."

2   Psalms 84.2: "My soul longeth, yea, even fainteth for the courts of the Lord. My heart and my flesh crieth out for the living God." (KJV) This psalm is closely associated with the 9th of Av, commemorating the destruction of the Temple.

6   Exodus 19.4: "Ye have seen what I did unto the Egyptians, and how I bore you on eagles' wings, and brought you unto myself."

Can Lifeless Bodies (*p.* 104)

[Brody II, pp. 184–7]

The Arabic superscription in the *diwan* reads: "And he said after many insisted that he remain in Andalusia." The Hebrew scholar, Joseph Yahalom, however, based on his reading of the superscription in the "New *Diwan*" in the Firkovitch Collection in St. Petersburg, and the poet's own description of a desert crossing toward the end of the first section, has suggested that the poem was written in Egypt after trying to reach the Holy Land by an overland, desert route used by pilgrims. A strophic *meruba* [see notes to section 7 of "On The Sea"] rhyming *aaaa, bbba, ccca, ddda*, etc.

5   Genesis 27.46: "I am weary of my life because of the daughter of Heth."

11   Cf. this line and what follows with Gabirol's poem, "What's Troubling You, My Soul", lines 55–60. See Cole, *Selected Poems of Solomon Ibn Gabirol* (Princeton: Princeton University Press, 2001), p. 86.

15   Song of Songs 4:8: ". . . look from the top of Amana, from the top of Senir and Hermon, from the lions' den, from the mountains of the leopards."

25   Isaiah 33.14: ". . . Who among us shall dwell with the devouring fire? Who among us shall dwell with everlasting burnings?"

28–9 Psalms 104:8: "They go up by the mountains; they go down by the valleys . . ." (KJV)

38   Exodus 4.10: "O my lord, I am not eloquent." Everett Fox renders this literally as "No man of words am I."

42   "Drunkards" is Schirmann's reading of this line, but Dov Yarden's reading of "hirelings" is equally plausible.

46   Literally, service to *Asherim*, Phonecian goddess of prosperity.

47–8 Job 40.29: "Wilt thou play with him as with a bird? Or wilt thou bind him for thy maidens?"

51–2 Philistines, Hagarites and Hittites, here standing for Berbers, Muslims and Christians.

66–70 The Ark of the Covenant and the tablets were traditionally believed to be buried before the destruction of the First Temple in or near Kiryat Yearim.

108 Genesis 4.12: "When thou tills the ground, it shall not henceforth yield unto thee her strength; a fugitive and a wanderer shalt thou be in the earth."

113 Job 13.26: "That Thou shouldest write bitter things against me, and make me to inhereit the iniquities of my youth."

117–8 Lamentations 3.22–23: "That the Lord's mercies are not consumed, and that His compassions fail not. They are new every morning: great is Thy faithfulness."

119 In the Hebrew "answer", *tshova*, can also mean penitence. Jeremiah 3.12: "Return thou backsliding Israel."

121 Genesis 37.30: "And he returned unto his brethren, and said: 'The child is not; and as for me, wither shall I go?'"

128 Isaiah 55.7: "And let him return unto the Lord, and He will have mercy upon him; and to our God, for He will abundantly pardon."

134 Nehemiah 9.13: "Thou camest down also upon mount Sinai, and spakest with them from heaven, and gavest them right judgements . . ."

Primed for Flight (*p.* 108)

[Brody II, pp. 160–3]

The Arabic superscription in the *diwan* reads: "And he said of the sea." The poem should be read while keeping verses 23–32 of Psalm 107 in mind. Traditionally believed to have been composed in Spain shortly before sailing for Alexandria, it is equally plausible that "Primed for Flight" was written in Alexandria, as the poet prepared himself for the final leg of his voyage to Palestine. Halevi's application of images based on such neo-Platonic ideas as purification, illumination and union are discussed in András Hamori, 'Lights in the Heart of the Sea: Some Images of Judah Halevi's', *Journal of Semitic Studies*, XXX.1, Spring 1985, pp. 75–83.

6 Judges 18.9: ". . . be not slothful to go and to enter in to possess the land."

7 Genesis 25.29–34: Jacob gives away his pottage to Esau in exchange for the latter's birthright. Proverbs 30.16: ". . . and the fire that saith not, 'Enough.'"

12 Psalms 12.3: "With flattering lip, and with a double heart, do they speak."

15   Psalms 46.3: "Therefore will we not fear, though the earth change, and though the mountains be moved in the midst of the sea."

26   Jeremiah 8.17: "For, behold, I will send serpents, cockatrices, among you, which will not be charmed, and they shall bite you, saith the Lord."

27–8 Isaiah 33.23: "Thy tacklings are loosed; they could not strengthen the socket of their mast, they could not spread the sail . . ."

34   Job 41.21: "Clubs are counted as stubble: he laugheth at the rattling of the javelin."

40   Jeremiah 17.1: "The sins of Judah is written with a pen of iron, and with the point of a diamond: it is graven upon the table of their heart, and upon the horns of your altars."

49   Psalms 107.29: "He maketh the storm a calm, so that the waves thereof are still."

50   1 Samuel 30.16: "And when he had brought him down, behold, they were spread abroad upon the earth . . ."

52   Psalms 45.14: "All glorious is the king's daughter within the palace; her raiment is of chequer work inwrought with gold."

61–2 Psalms 89.10: "Thou rulest the proud swelling of the sea; when the waves thereof arise, Thou stillest them."

My Heart is in the East (p. 110)

[Brody II, p. 155]

Nostalgia for one's historic homeland in the east was also a prevalent theme among the Hispano-Arabic poets of Andalusia. The source of this poem may have originated in the Arabic poem by Abd-ar-Rahman (756–788), the first Emir of Andalusia:

> A palm tree I beheld in Ar-Rusafa,
> far in the West, far from the palm-tree land;
> I said: You, like myself, are far away, in a strange land;
> how long have I been far away from my people!
> You grew up in a land where you are a stranger,
> and like myself, are living in the farthest corner of the earth:
> may the morning clouds refresh you at this distance,
> and may abundant rains comfort you forever!

3   Numbers 30.5: "And her father heareth her vow, or her bond wherewith she hath bound her soul, and her father holdeth his peace at her, then all her vows shall stand, and every bond wherewith she hath bound her soul shall stand."

4   Edom: after the occupation of Palestine by the Crusaders (1099); Arabia: Muslim Spain.

7   Psalms 28.2: "Hear the voice of my supplications, when I cry

unto Thee, when I lift up my hands toward Thy holy Sanctuary."

On the Sea (*p.* 111)

1 [Brody II, p. 168]

1   Psalms 93.4: "Above the voices of many waters, the mighty breakers of the sea, the Lord on high is mighty."

2   Isaiah 44.27: "That saith to the deep, *Be dry,* and I will dry up thy rivers."

3   Psalms 138.2: "I will bow down toward Thy holy temple, and give thanks unto Thy name for Thy mercy and for Thy truth; for Thou has magnified Thy word above all Thy name."

7   Psalms 20.6: "We will shout for joy in thy victory, and in the name of our God we will set up our standards; the Lord fulfil all thy petitions." Psalms 102.28: "But Thou are the selfsame, and Thy years shall have no end."

8   Genesis 43.9: "I will be surety for him; of my hand shalt thou require him . . ."

2 [Brody II, p. 169]

1   Genesis 6.17: "And I, behold, I do bring the flood of waters upon the earth . . ."

2–3   Jeremiah 33.10: "Thus saith the Lord: Yet again there shall be heard in this place, whereof ye say: It is waste, without man and without beast . . ." Genesis 7.21: "All flesh perished that moved upon the earth, both fowl, and cattle, and beast . . ."

4   Isaiah 50.11: "This shall ye have of My hand; Ye shall lie down in sorrow." *Ma'atseva,* translated here as sorrow, is derived from the root *etsev,* whose sense is pain, hurt, toil; thus the most recent (1985) JPS translation of the Bible, *Tanakh,* renders the line: "You shall lie down in pain."

6   Jeremiah 2.6: "Through a land of deserts and of pits . . ." The word for pit, *shucha,* is derived from *shuch*: 'to sink down, to melt away, to vanish', hence my own choice of "shifting sands"; it is unlikely that a pit or depression would have been sighted from aboard ship.

12   Job 41.23: "He maketh the deep to boil like a pot; He maketh the sea like a seething mixture."

3 [Brody II, p. 170]

The superscription in the *diwan* reads: "And he said of the frightful surging of the sea and of his yearnings for his family."

2   From the prayer concluding the Jewish daily service, *Alenu:* "We bend the knee and bow and acknowledge before the supreme

King of kings . . ."

6–7   1 Kings 8.7: "For the cherubim spread forth their wings over the place of the ark . . ." Zechariah 5.9: "Then I lifted my eyes, and saw, and behold, there came forth two women, and the wind was in their wings; for they had wings like the wings of a stork . . ."

9   Isaiah 16.11: "Wherefore my heart moaneth like a harp for Moab, and mine inward parts for Kir-heres."

11   Numbers 24.24: "And the ships shall come from the coast of Kittim . . ."

16–18   Jeremiah 4.31: "For I have heard a voice as of a woman in travail, the anguish as of her that bringeth forth her first child . . ."

26–7   Judges 11.34: "And Jephthah came to Mitzpah unto his house, and, behold, his daughter came out to meet him with timbrels and with dances; and she was his only child . . ." Halevi's evocation of Jephthah and his daughter, who was sacrificed by her own father, lends an especially somber coloring to this passage.

33–4   Psalms 100.4: "Enter into His gates with thanksgiving, and into His courts with praise . . ."

39   Genesis 21.30: "And he said, For these seven ewe lambs shalt thou take of my hand, that they may be a witness unto me, that I have digged this well."

4 [Brody II, pp. 174–5]

The superscription in the *diwan* reads: "And he said in the midst of a storm."

1   Nahum 2.11: "She is empty, and void, and waste: and the heart melteth, and knees smite together, and much pain is in all loins . . ."

4   Psalms 76.5: "The stout hearted are spoiled, they have slept their sleep: and none of the men of might have found their hands." (KJV)

8   Psalms 107.27: "They reel to and fro, and stagger like a drunken man . . ."

9   Psalms 116.19: "In the courts of the Lord's home, in the midst of thee, O Jerusalem."

5 [Brody II, pp. 172–4]

The superscription in the *diwan* reads: "And he said of his yearnings for his family and homeland."

1   Job 32.18: "For I am full of words; the spirit within me constraineth me." Psalms 42.3: "My soul thirsteth for God, for the living God . . ."

2   Psalms 122.5: "For there were set thrones for judgment, the thrones of the house of David." Psalms 105:15: "Touch not Mine anointed ones, and do My prophets no harm."

3   Genesis 31.28: "And hast not suffered me to kiss my sons and my daughters?"

5–6   Ecclesiastes 2.5–6: "I made me gardens and parks, and I planted trees in them of all kinds of fruits; I made me pools of water, to water therefrom the wood springing up with trees." Schirmann has suggested that Halevi is alluding here to his own circle of students in Andalusia.

10   Deuteronomy 33.34: "And for the precious things of the fruits of the sun, and for the precious things of the yield of the moons . . ." The quoted passage is from Moses' blessing the children of Israel before his death. The verse is part of the blessing to Joseph.

16–18   Isaiah 42.8: "I am the Lord, that is My name; and My glory will I not give to another, neither My praise to graven images."

20   Genesis 22.13: "And Abraham lifted up his eyes, and looked, and behold behind him a ram caught in the thicket by his thorns."

21   Song of Songs 4.14: "Spikenard and saffron, calamus and cinnamon, will all trees of frankincense; myrrh and aloes, with all the chief spices."

24   Isaiah 43.16: "Thus saith the Lord, who maketh a way in the sea, and a path in the mighty waters." Ezekiel 27.4: "Thy borders are in the heart of the seas . . ."

27   1 Samuel 1.15: "Hannah answered and said: 'No, my lord, I am a woman of a sorrowful spirit; I have drunk neither wine nor strong drink, but I poured out my soul before the Lord.'"

32   Exodus 23.20: "Behold, I send an angel before thee, to keep thee by the way, and to bring thee into the place which I have prepared."

33   Psalms 69.31: "I will praise the name of God with a song . . ."

6 [Brody II, p. 174]

The superscription in the *diwan* reads: "And he said in the midst of a storm."

2   Psalms 93.3: "The floods have lifted up, O Lord, the floods have lifted up their voice; the floods lift up their roaring."

4   Psalms 95.5: "The sea is His, and He made it . . ."

5   Daniel 6.27: "For He is the living God, and steadfast for ever . . ."

8   Jeremiah 5.22: "Who have placed the sand for the bound of the sea . . ."

7 [Brody II, pp. 176–9]

A *me'ora*. The poem is written in the form of the Andalusian *meruba* ("square"), a strophic poem, most often applied to secular themes, in which each section is made up of seven strophes, each strophe consisting of four short lines rhyming *aaab, cccb, dddb, eeeb*, etc. The acrostic

Yehuda is formed out of the initial letter of each section.

2 Isaiah 14.24: "And as I have purposed, so shall it stand . . ."

5–7 Jeremiah 10.23: "O Lord, I know that man's way is not his own; it is not in man to direct his steps as he walketh."

13–14 Psalms 19.6: "And rejoiceth as a strong man to run his course."

21 Daniel 8.22: "And as for that which was broken, in the place whereof four stood up, four kingdoms shall stand up out of the nation, but not with his power."

28–30 Psalms 139.7: "Whither shall I go from Thy spirit? Or whither shall I flee from Thy presence?"

31 Jeremiah 5.22: ". . . And though the waves thereof toss themselves, yet can they not prevail; though they roar, yet can they not pass over it."

32–3 Isaiah 19.1: "Behold, the Lord rideth upon a swift cloud, and cometh unto Egypt . . ."

38–9 Job 41.23: "He maketh the deep to boil like a pot . . ." Isaiah 42.13: "He will cry, yea, He will shout aloud . . ."

45–6 Psalms 107.26: "They mounted up to the heaven, they went down to the deeps . . ." This psalm, particularly the section describing "God's care of sea-voyagers" (verses 23–32), is central to Halevi's entire sequence of sea poems.

52–3 Psalms 18.17: "He sent from on high, He took me; He drew me out of many waters."

55 Isaiah 1.14: "Your new moons and your appointed feasts My soul hateth; they are a burden unto Me; I am weary to bear them."

56–7 Job 38.24: "But what way is the light parted, or the east wind scattered upon the earth?" Psalms 29.5: "The voice of the Lord breaketh the cedars . . ."

71–2 Isaiah 56.10: "His watchmen are all blind . . ."

72–3 Genesis 27.12: "My father peradventure will feel me, and I shall seem to him as a mocker . . ."

74–5 Psalms 44.13: "Thou sellest Thy people for small gain . . ."

82–4 2 Kings 14.26: "For the Lord saw the affliction of Israel, that it was very bitter; for there was none shut up nor left at large . . ."

85 Isaiah 38.14: "Mine eyes fail with looking upward . . ."

93–4 Psalms 104.34: "Let my musings be sweet unto him . . ." Isaiah: 23.16: "Make sweet melody, sing many songs . . ."

100 Nehemiah 9.25: ". . . so they did eat, and were filled, and became fat, and luxuriated in Thy great goodness."

101–2 Exodus 15.23–25: "And when they came to Marah, they could not drink of the waters of Marah, for they were bitter. Therefore the name of it was called Marah. And the people murmured against Moses, saying: 'What shall we drink?' And he cried unto the Lord; and the Lord showed him a tree, and he cast it into the waters, and the waters were made sweet."

106–8 Isaiah 43.16: "Thus saith the Lord, which maketh a way in the sea, and a path in the mighty waters."

110 Job 37.10: "By the breath of God ice is given . . ."

112 Psalms 106.23: "Therefore He said that He would destroy them, had not Moses His chosen stood before Him in the breach, to turn back His wrath, lest He should destroy him."

112–6 Psalms 116.16: ". . . I am Thy servant, the son of Thy handmaid; Thou has loosed my bands." S.D. Goitein notes in *The Mediterranean Society* (Berkeley: University of California Press, Vol. 5, 1988) that in Halevi's day the small boats, used to convey passengers to their ships anchored offshore, were called "handmaids". Literally, "He has turned his wrath/from the son of his handmaid/and redeemed his soul from *sheol* [the underworld]."

124–5 Job 30.25: ". . . was not my soul grieved for the poor?" 2 Samuel 5.24: "And it shall be, when thou hearest the sound of marching in the tops of the mulberry-trees, that then thou shalt bestir thyself . . ."

134–5 Isaiah 60.1: "Arise, shine; for thy light is come, and the glory of the Lord is risen upon thee."

8 [Brody II, pp. 175–6]

2–3 Zechariah 9.12: "Return to the stronghold, Ye prisoners of hope . . ."

4 Psalms 31.6: "Into Thy hand I commit my spirit . . ."

7–8 1 Samuel 20.3: ". . . but truly as the Lord liveth, and as thy soul liveth, there is but a step between me and death."

10 The minimum required, according to Jewish law, for burial; also traditionally the four cubits of the law.

15 Job 30.12: "Upon my right hand rise the youth . . ."

17–18 Ecclesiastes 9.11: "I returned, and saw under the sun, that the race is not to the swift, nor the battle to the strong, neither yet bread to the wise, nor yet riches to men of understanding, nor yet favor to men of skill . . ."

20 Psalms 51.8: "Behold, thou desirest truth in the inward parts . . ." Psalms 28.7: "Therefore my heart greatly rejoiceth . . ."

22 Psalms 42.5: "These things I remember, and pour out my soul within me, how I passed on with the throng, and led them to the house of God . . ."

23 From the Benediction on Deliverance, recited upon completion of a voyage: "Blessed art Thou, Lord our God, King of the universe, who bestowest favors on the undeserving, and has shown me every kindness."

9 [Brody II, pp. 171–2]

3   Psalms 135.7: "He bringeth forth the wind out of His treasuries."
4–6   Jeremiah 34.17: ". . . behold, I proclaim for you a liberty, saith the
      Lord . . ." Song of Songs 1.13: "My beloved is unto me a bundle
      of myrrh which lieth betwixt my breasts." For the multiple
      senses of myrrh, *dror*, cf. the note to "Admonitions", 1.
10   Joshua 10.6: "Slack not thy hands from thy servants . . ."
13   Psalms 106.9: "And He rebuked the Red Sea, and it was dried
      up . . ."
14   Jeremiah 1.13: "And the word of the Lord came unto me the
      second time, saying: 'What seest thou?' And I said: 'I see a
      seething pot; and the face thereof is from the north.'"
18–19 Amos 4.13: "For, lo, He that formeth the mountains, and
      createth the wind, and declareth unto man what is his thought,
      that maketh the morning darkness, and treadeth upon the high
      places of the earth; the Lord, the God of hosts, is His name."

Egypt (*p.* 121)
[Brody II, p. 180]

1   Ezekiel 38.11: ". . . I will go up against the land of unwalled
      villages . . ."
5   Matronita: *Shekhinah.* Name given to the Divine Presence by
      the thirteenth-century Spanish-Hebrew Kabbalist, Moshe de
      Leon, author of the *Zohar.* I have taken the liberty of using the
      appellation anachronistically on account of its aural appeal and
      connotative value, wherein the feminine, queen-like, and moth-
      erly aspects of the Shekhinah are made apparent to the English
      reader.
5–6   Exodus 11.4: "And Moses said, Thus said the Lord: About
      midnight will I go out into the midst of Egypt . . ." Exodus
      12.23: "For the Lord will pass though to smite the Egyptians;
      and when he seeth the blood upon the lintel, and on the two side
      posts, the Lord will pass over the door . . ."
7   Exodus 13.21–22: "And the Lord went before them by day in a
      pillar of cloud, to lead them the way; and by night in a pillar of
      fire, to give them light . . ."
9   Isaiah 51.1: "Look unto the rock whence ye were hewn . . ."
      Moses and Aaron were born in Egypt.
10   "Leaders", *pinot*, or "corners", perhaps in the sense of "corner-
      stones." Judges 20.2: "And the chiefs of all the people, *even* of all
      the tribes of Israel, presented themselves in the assembly of the
      people of God . . ."

To His Friend and Host Ibn al-Ammani (*p.* 122)

See introduction for information concerning Aharon Ibn al-Ammani, chief *dayan* of Alexandria and Halevi's principal host during his sojourn in Egypt.

1 [Brody II, pp. 257–8]

4　Psalms 16.6: "The lines are fallen unto me in pleasant places."

5　Proverbs 8.30: "Then I was by Him, as a nursling . . ." Amon was the tutelary deity of No (Thebes), which stood for Egypt in Medieval Hebrew poetry. Nahum, 3.8: "Art thou better than No-amon, that was situate among the rivers . . ."

14　Song of Songs 8.14: "Make haste, my beloved, and be thou like to a gazelle, or to a young hart upon the mountains of spices." The last lines of the Song of Songs have been subject to extensive exegesis. Thus the Midrash reads: "Mayest Thou hasten the advent of the redemption and cause the *Shekhinah* to dwell on the mountain of spices and rebuild the Temple speedily in our days." See also note to line 36 of "On Parting from his Friend Moshe Ibn Ezra".

15　Law, or Torah, i.e., religious and moral instruction.

16　Literally, *Urim* and *Tummim*. Exodus 28.30: "And thou shalt put in the breastplate of judgement the Urim and Thummin; and they shall be upon Aaron's heart, when he goeth in before the Lord . . ." Of the Urim and Tummin Everett Fox writes, in *The Five Books of Moses* (London: The Harvill Press, 1995, p. 418), "Oracular objects for divining God's plans (e.g. learning if it was the right time to go into battle). Their exact shape and mode of operation are the subject of much scholarly debate . . . In Samuel 28.6 *Urim* are equated with dreams and prophets as a means of answering human queries . . . It is worth noting that *Urim* begins with the first letter of the Hebrew alphabet, and *Tummin* the last, giving rise to the possibility that the names themselves are symbols."

2 [Brody I, pp. 10–11]

Joseph Yahalom has argued persuasively that this short lyric was written on ship anchored off the port of Alexandria as Halevi waited for favorable winds to take him to Acre on the northern coast of Palestine (and not, as Goitien assumed from the Arabic superscription, on board ship while waiting to enter Alexandria for the first time). It is, according to Yahalom, a companion-piece to "Break not, Lord, the breakers of the sea . . .", and yet its tone betrays seemingly contrary currents of emotions: whereas the latter poem praises the west wind for finally filling the ships sails, in "Stop the surging of the sea . . .", Halevi is overwhelmed by the thought of having to leave his Alexandrian friend and begs the winds to calm down so that he can row back to shore and kiss the hand of al-Ammani. It is only in the poem's last couplet that the poet pulls himself together and imagines lounging in the "great king's city" as a just reward for leaving the comforts of his friend's home, which he compares to "the balms of Gilead". See Joseph Yahalom, "The Leningrad Geniza and Research on the Poetry of Yehuda Halevi", [Hebrew] *Pe'amim: Studies in Oriental Jewry*, Vol. 46–47, Spring 1991, pp. 55–74.

3   Sceptre, or rod, but also in Hebrew "tribe", as in the tribes of Israel.

4   Deuteronomy 34.7: "And Moses *was* an hundred and twenty years old when he died; his eye was not dim, nor his natural force abated."

5   Proverbs 30.15: ". . . There are three things that are never satisfied, yea, four that say not: 'Enough.'"

9–10   Jeremiah 8.22: "Is there no balm in Gilead?"

11   Nehemiah 8.15: "Go forth unto the mount, and fetch olive branches, and branches of wild olive, and myrtle branches, and palm branches, and branches of thick trees, to make a booth, as it is written." Halevi seeks the shade of a "thick branch", which has been traditionally interpreted as a species of myrtle.

14   Psalms 48.3: ". . . The city of the great king."

Fate Has Flung Me (*p.* 124)

[Brody II, p. 182]

The superscription in the *diwan* reads: "And he said of the Egyptian desert." This short poem of extreme concision plays on the verb-stem *sanaf*, "to wrap", or "wind", which is used in slightly altered grammatical forms as the first and last word of the poem (as well as appearing as the end-rhyme of the second line). Both Schirmann and Yarden gloss the last line, "I will wear the hat of his holiness like a turban" taking their cue from Leviticus 16.4: "He shall wind [his head] with the turban." I have opted for what appears to have greater contextual validity, in which donning "the splendor of his holiness" the poet imagines himself joyfully whirling round like a dervish.

1–2   Isaiah 22.17–18: "Behold, the Lord will hurl thee up and down with a man's throw; Yea, He will wind thee round and round; He will violently roll and toss thee like a ball into a large country."

4   Cf. Halevi's poem "Earth's Delight and Sovereign City." Psalms 48.3: "Fair in situation, the joy of the whole earth; even mount Zion, the uttermost parts of the north, the city of the great King . . ."

4   Elohi: My God.

In Alexandria (*p.* 125)

[Brody I, p. 112]

The opening section of a *qasida*, replying to a letter from Halevi's friend in Cairo, Nathan Ibn Shmuel (court secretary to the Egyptian *Nagid* Shmuel ben Hananya). Thanks to the extensive documentation uncovered in the Cairo Geniza concerning Halevi's activities during his sojourn in Egypt, we know this lyric to have been composed between October and December 1140.

1   Ezekiel 26.16: "Then all the princes of the sea shall come down from their thrones, and lay away their robes, and strip-off their richly woven garments; they shall clothe themselves with trembling . . ."

6   Goshen: Egypt, or its northern delta area. Genesis 45.10: "And thou shalt dwell in the land of Goshen . . ."

7–8   Exodus 28.8: "And the curious girdle of the ephod [breastplate], which is upon it, shall be of the same, according to the work thereof; even of gold, of blue, and purple, and scarlet, and fine twined linen."

15   The river Nile was frequently referred to as the Pishon. Genesis 2.11: "And the name of the first is Pishon: that is it which compasseth the whole land of Havilah, where there is gold."

18   Psalms 45.14–15: "All glorious is the king's daughter within the palace; her raiment is of chequer work inwrought with gold. She shall be led unto the king on richly woven stuff; the virgins her companions in her train being brought unto thee." Cf. "Primed for Flight", line 52.

Poetica

A series of texts, translations and miscellaneous poetic works

1 THE POEMS OF MELEAGER
   Peter Whigham and Peter Jay
2 THE NOISE MADE BY POEMS *Peter Levi*
3 THE SATIRES OF PERSIUS *W. S. Merwin*
4 FLOWER AND SONG: Aztec Poems *Edward Kissam*
   & Michael Schmidt
5 PALLADAS: Poems *Tony Harrison*
11 OLD ENGLISH RIDDLES *Michael Alexander*
12 AN UNOFFICIAL RILKE (Poems 1912–1926)
   Michael Hamburger
14 MARTIAL: Letter to Juvenal *Peter Whigham*
15 LI HE: Goddesses, Ghosts, and Demons *J. D. Frodsham*
16 NIETZSCHE: Dithyrambs of Dionysus *R. J. Hollingdale*
17 POEMS OF JULES LAFORGUE *Peter Dale*
18 GÉRARD DE NERVAL: The Chimeras *Peter Jay*
   & Richard Holmes
19 THE LAMENTATION OF THE DEAD *Peter Levi*
20 APOLLINAIRE: Selected Poems *Oliver Bernard*
21 SLOW CHRYSANTHEMUMS: Classical Korean Poetry
   in Chinese *Kim Jong-gil*
22 RIMBAUD: A Season in Hell and Other Poems
   Norman Cameron
23 THE SELECTED POEMS OF TU FU *David Hinton*
24 HÖLDERLIN: Poems and Fragments *Michael Hamburger*
25 LUIS DE GONGORA: Selected Shorter Poems
   Michael Smith
26 BORROWED WARE: Medieval Persian Epigrams
   Dick Davis
27 SAPPHO THROUGH ENGLISH POETRY
   Peter Jay and Caroline Lewis (eds.)
28 THE TRUTH OF POETRY *Michael Hamburger*
29 GOETHE: Roman Elegies and other poems
   Michael Hamburger
30 DANTE: THE DIVINE COMEDY *Peter Dale*
31 THE SELECTED POEMS OF LI PO *David Hinton*

For details of these and our other books, please visit our website:
www.anvilpresspoetry.com